Greatest Moments

Sports Illustrated

Greatest Moments

in sports history

ISBN: 1-929049-01-3
Manufactured in the United States of America
First printing 2000

Library of Congress Catalog Number: 00-101695

SPORTS ILLUSTRATED Director of Development: STANLEY WEIL

GREATEST MOMENTS IN SPORTS HISTORY

Editorial Director: MORIN BISHOP
  Project Editor: JOHN BOLSTER
  Managing Editor: JEANANN PANNASCH
  Reporters/Writers: WARD CALHOUN, THERESA DEAL, JEFF LABRECQUE, MERRELL NODEN, YLANN SCHEMM
  Photography Editor: JOHN S. BLACKMAR
Designers: BARBARA CHILENSKAS, VINCENT MEJIA

GREATEST MOMENTS IN SPORTS HISTORY was prepared by
Bishop Books, Inc.
611 Broadway
New York, New York 10012

TIME INC. HOME ENTERTAINMENT
President Stuart Hotchkiss
Executive Director, Branded Businesses David Arfine
Executive Director, Non Branded Businesses Alicia Longobardo
Executive Director, Time Inc. Brand Licensing Risa Turken
Director, Licensing Scott Rosenzweig
Executive Director, Marketing Services Carol Pittard
Director, Retail & Special Sales Tom Mifsud
Director, Branded Businesses Maarten Terry
Associate Directors Roberta Harris, Kenneth Maehlum
Product Managers Dana Gregory, Andre Okolowitz, Ann Marie Ross, Niki Viswanathan, Daria Raehse
Associate Product Managers Victoria Alfonso, Jennifer Dowell, Dennis Sheehan, Meredith Shelley, Lauren Zaslansky
Assistant Product Managers Ann Gillespie, Meredith Peters, Virginia Valdes
Telemarketing Manager Marina Weinstein
Associate Manager, e-Commerce Dima Masrizada
Licensing Manager Joanna West
Associate Licensing Manager Regina Feiler
Licensing Coordinator Laury Shapiro
Associate Manager, Retail & New Markets Bozena Szwagulinski
Coordinator, Retail Marketing Gina Di Meglio
Editorial Operations Director John Calvano
Assitant Editorial Operations Manager Emily Rabin
Book Production Manager Jessica McGrath
Associate Book Production Manager Jonathan Polsky
Assistant Book Production Manager Suzanne DeBenedetto
Fulfillment Manager Richard Perez
Assistant Fulfillment Manager Tara Schimming
Financial Director Tricia Griffin
Financial Manager Robert Dente
Associate Financial Manager Steven Sandonato
Assistant Financial Manager Tamara Whittier
Executive Assistant Mary Jane Rigoroso

We welcome your comments and suggestions about SPORTS ILLUSTRATED Books.
Please write to us at:
SPORTS ILLUSTRATED
Attention: Book Editors
PO Box 11016
Des Moines, IA 50336-1016

If you would like to order any of our Hard Cover Collector Edition books, please call us at 1-800-327-6388.
(Monday through Friday, 7:00 a.m.– 8:00 p.m. or Saturday, 7:00 a.m.– 6:00 p.m. Central Time).

10 9 8 7 6 5 4 3 2 1

Contents

Introduction

Here, at the end of the first century of sport, we look back in amazement at the astonishing 100 years just past. One hundred years ago, the modern Olympic Games were only four years old, the first World Series was still three years away, and professional sports leagues like the NFL, NBA and NHL were decades away from existence. If you were lucky enough to be a man in 1900 and a member of the upper class, you no doubt had some notion of sport as a character-building activity, one of the ingredients that made up a well-rounded man. But you most likely would have thought of "sport" as hunting or fishing or an individual endeavor such as equestrianism, sculling or swimming. Team sports—and especially team sports contested for paying spectators—were hardly the force they now are.

But as saturated in sports culture as we are today, sports nourish us in several important ways. To begin with, they are a communal experience. More than any book or play—

more than just about any movie—sports are a source of shared memories, images that linger in our collective mind: Michael Jordan flying to the basket; the spindly legs of Babe Ruth beneath his round body; Willie Mays's back— No. 24—as he chases down Vic Wertz's fly ball in the Polo Grounds. All of these images feed our imagination, for in a world of hard probabilities, we still look to sports for proof that miracles happen.

We have chosen 60 moments to celebrate as the greatest in the first century of sport, and we make honorable mention of 15 more. Our pages contain two Babes (Ruth and Didrikson), one Woods (Tiger) and a host of miracles—on ice, in the mud and through the air. We've divided them into four categories— Gamewinners, Legendmakers, Recordbreakers and Stunners—but our definitions are fairly fluid. Many of the moments we've chosen could easily qualify in more than one category. Bobby Thomson's dramatic home

Jordan's career is studded with great moments.

Joe Namath's greatest accomplishment came in Super Bowl III.

Secretariat stunned horse racing with his 31-length victory in the 1973 Belmont.

run that sent the Giants to the 1951 World Series, for example, was a gamewinning home run, but it's such a landmark moment that we put it in Legendmakers. The Miracle of Coogan's Bluff, as sportswriter Red Smith dubbed it, was so dramatic we could have put it in Stunners, for that matter, but you get the idea: The categories are not set in stone, but they cover a century of great sports moments.

On what basis have we made our choices? For the Stunners section, certainly, one crucial ingredient is shock—the extent to which an event defied our expectations. We might call this the "David Factor" in honor of history's first great underdog, the shepherd boy with the deadly sling. However eagerly we might anticipate a clash of Goliaths, there is nothing like seeing one laid low by an unheralded rival. Our book is full of Davids. Who would

have guessed that little-known Buster Douglas, a 35–1 longshot, could knock out the seemingly invincible Mike Tyson in 1990? Or that the Miracle Mets of 1969, only seven years removed from their disastrous debut season, would rally for the NL pennant and defeat the favored Orioles in the World Series?

Sports fans crave surprise. Indeed, real suspense was the one thing Carl Lewis couldn't deliver at the 1984 Olympic Games in Los Angeles, when he matched Jesse Owens's feat of winning four gold medals in a single Olympics. No wonder Lewis didn't emerge from those Games an unequivocal hero: To anyone who really knew track and field, the only shock would have been for him to fail.

Lewis's fate might have been different had he broken a world record or two, for we also reserve a special place in our list for those who

Mark Spitz (center) won seven gold medals and set seven world records at the 1972 Olympics in Munich.

do the impossible—or better, who extend the boundaries of the possible. For years and years, knowledgable people argued that it was physically impossible for a man to run the mile in fewer than four minutes. So perhaps it made sense that when that august barrier finally fell, on May 6, 1954, it was to Roger Bannister, a medical student, who ran with a scientist's clear-eyed understanding of the human body's limits. Not so Bob Beamon, who at the 1968 Olympics in Mexico City broke the world record in the long jump by a staggering 21¾ inches, leaping with legs splayed right past the 28- and 29-foot barriers to touch down at 29'2½". Talk about great

leaps for mankind: The realization of what he'd done, not the doing of it, sapped the energy from Beamon's legs, and he fell to his knees in what Bannister might have recognized as a "cataplectic seizure."

Another factor that determines whether an event lodges in our imagination is historical context. Here, we sports fans have much to answer for: We have always invested games and competitions with far more meaning than they should ever be asked to bear. The Cold War was a magnifying glass through which both sides viewed every clash between the U.S. and the Soviet Union. The U.S. Olympic hockey team's shocker over the

Soviets at Lake Placid was a prime example of this. Was it, as some said, a victory for the American way of life over Communism? More likely it was just one hell of an upset.

No one, of course, was more ready to use sport as propaganda than Adolf Hitler, who promoted the 1936 Olympics as a vindication of his theories of Aryan racial superiority. Whether he liked it or not, Jesse Owens could hardly have asked for a bigger stage than the one awaiting him in Berlin.

A little controversy doesn't hurt, either. In some cases, it's a veritable preservative, immortalizing by stimulating debate. Did Babe Ruth really "call" his shot off Chicago Cubs pitcher Charlie Root in the 1932 World Series, or was he merely pointing to one of the Cubs, who had been riding him mercilessly throughout the game? We'll probably never know.

When it comes to such legendary moments, we are all editors, lopping off facts that don't quite fit the myth as we want to remember it. Who, for example, doesn't have to think for a second to recall that Carlton Fisk's Boston Red Sox lost the 1975 World Series after his dramatic home run in Game 6? Who remembers that Bobby Riggs was 55 years old on the day of his gender-war tennis match with Billie Jean King?

Finally, let's hear it for the chroniclers—writers, radio men and spectators—all of whom play a crucial part in passing this stuff down to us. There's nothing like a little poetry to bring history to life. So here's to Pittsburgh broadcaster Myron Cope, who was willing to risk an eternity in hell to publicize the splendid moniker The Immaculate Reception, which a fan had suggested to him. And here's to Celtics announcer Johnny Most, whose screeching "Havlicek stole the ball! Havlicek stole the ball!" did not win him any prizes for

Golden moment: At 46, Nicklaus won the '86 Masters.

objective reporting, but probably did as much to immortalize that play as Havlicek did.

The commentators amplified these moments, but the athletes in these pages made them, and we thank those men and women for the things they've shown us, moments of surpassing courage and grace, all of which keep the world a fresh and surprising place.

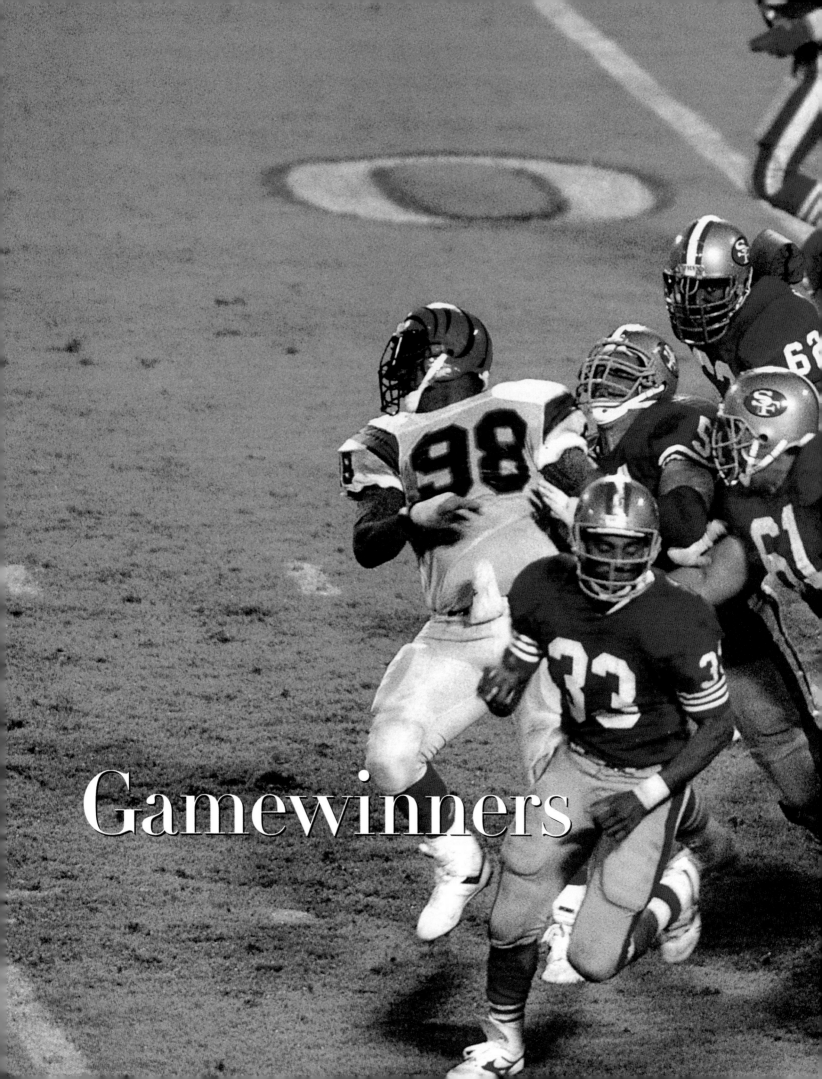

Gamewinners

Introduction

Diego Maradona put Argentina on top of the world in 1986.

In addition to being the pivotal moments of crucial contests, the plays in our Gamewinners section have one thing in common: They are seared into the memory of every sports fan. They come in several forms, from the utterly improbable (Steeler running back Franco Harris's Immaculate Reception against Oakland in 1972) to the thoroughly dominant (Chicago guard Michael Jordan's incredible flourish at the end of Game 6 of the 1998 NBA Finals) to the sadly inadequate (Bills' kicker Scott Norwood's missed field goal against the Giants in the waning seconds of Super Bowl XXV), but they are all equally memorable—and remembered. Even the casual sports fan recalls Boston catcher Carlton Fisk urging the ball fair as he

hopped, skipped and jumped down the first base line after hitting the winning home run against the Reds in Game 6 of the 1975 World Series. The sports junkie probably remembers where he was when the immortal shot left the park, and the Red Sox fan can tell you what she was wearing and what she had for breakfast that morning.

The unforgettable moments when the matter was settled, the championship won and lost—these are the plays you'll find in our Gamewinners section. Yet some were so important or astounding, or have assumed such a prominent position in the collective sporting consciousness, that they could just as easily go in our Legendmakers chapter. Boston College quarterback Doug Flutie's Hail Mary pass against

Both Gibson (above) and Dwight Clark (below) basked in unforgettable game-winning moments.

Miami in 1984, for instance; or Kirk Gibson's home run in the last of the ninth of Game 1 of the 1988 World Series against the A's. The clout won the game for Los Angeles, to be sure, but because of its particular circumstances—Gibson's injuries, his team's underdog status—it also entered Dodger legend.

Think of a historic, game-winning moment, and chances are you'll be able to read about it on the following pages. From Bill Mazeroski's Yankee-killing home run in Game 7 of the 1960 World Series—the first time the Series was ended by a home run—to Joe Carter's triumphant blast against the Phillies 33 years later—the second time the Series ended with a walk-off dinger. From Bobby Orr's Stanley Cup–winning goal against St. Louis in 1970—the NHL picked it as the greatest moment in league history—to Alan Ameche's NFL title–winning plunge in 1958. From Havlicek in '65 to Justin Leonard in '99, they're all here.

Okay, so Duke Blue Devil Christian Laettner's buzzer beater against Kentucky in the 1992 NCAA regional finals is *not* here. Our reasons? One, we only had 15 spots to fill, two, it wasn't a championship game and, three, while we realize that hindsight is 20/20, someone should have been fronting Laettner, or the passer, Grant Hill, on the play. That way Duke

doesn't have such an easy time completing a court-length inbounds pass. Also, didn't Laettner step on an opponent in that game, while the player was down? He did.

Sorry, Christian. But before Duke fans in Durham and across the country hit *send* on those million emails, we urge them to turn to page 170—that classic ending to a classic game made our Honorable Mention section.

The Catch

JANUARY 10, 1982 It's been replayed so many times that most fans can run it in slow-motion in their imaginations. The play ranks with the best of Joe Montana's fantastic finishes, which is saying something. No one in the Bay Area will ever forget Joe Cool's pass to his best friend Dwight Clark in the back of the end zone that January afternoon in 1982.

The NFC Championship game, a seesaw affair between the San Francisco 49ers and Dallas Cowboys, boiled down to one nailbiting play. Trailing 27–21 with 58 seconds left, Montana and the Niners were faced with a third-and-three on the Dallas six. Coach Bill Walsh gave his quarterback the play—Sprint Right Option—which called for Montana to roll out to his right and look for either wideout Freddie Solomon over the middle or Clark in the corner.

Montana ran to his right but quickly found his view, and his path, obstructed by the 6'9" Ed (Too Tall) Jones, among other Dallas linemen. He jumped and threw a pass toward the back of the end zone. In fact, the ball seemed destined for the first row. At that moment Clark, seeming to climb an invisible ladder, leaped up and snared the ball between his fingertips. He held on for the touchdown that sent the Niners to a 28–27 win and into their first Super Bowl. The play would pass into legend, known simply as The Catch.

THE OTHER SIDE

Among basketball players it's known as a "poster shot." No one wants to be the guy standing beneath the basket as Michael Jordan finishes a dunk and the cameras flash. In the deciding play of the 1981 NFC Championship game it was Dallas rookie defensive back Everson Walls who played the victim in the poster shot, frozen in time looking up helplessly as Dwight Clark makes the catch—or rather, The Catch.

Prior to the famous play, however, Walls was enjoying the game of his life. He'd intercepted two passes, recovered a fumble and made eight tackles. In fact, before The Catch, the 6'1" Walls seemed a clear choice for MVP of the game. In that one instant everything changed. Walls would later sign a copy of the *SI* cover photo to Clark with the tongue-in-cheek inscription: TO DWIGHT, YOU WERE OUT.

A solid cornerback with a knack for interceptions, Walls finished his career with 57 picks, tied for ninth on the NFL all-time list. He later made the cover of *Sports Illustrated* again. This time Walls was no poster shot victim, but a member of the 1990 Super Bowl Champion New York Giants.

Walls's dreaded "poster shot."

Saving His
Best For Last

JUNE 14, 1998 Michael Jordan's right hand lingered in the air even after the ball swished through the net, as if he was giving the Utah crowd a chance to piece their hearts back together and quickly take out their cameras to capture a piece of history. Such souvenirs, of course, would not be necessary. For those who witnessed the final moments of Game 6 of the 1998 NBA Finals, Jordan's championship-clinching shot—the last shot of his storybook career—would be burned into their minds forever: the perfect pose, the perfect player, the perfect ending.

The image will last. People will remember how Jordan shook Utah's defensive specialist Bryon Russell with a juke and a subtle nudge, the combination of which sent Russell to his knees, before calmly sinking the game-winner. But they might forget the other 43 points Jordan scored for Chicago that night, including the crucial layup he banked in with 37 seconds left. Or how he crept up on Karl Malone in the low post and stole the ball with 19 seconds on the clock and the Bulls trailing 86–85. In the end, they will remember the perfect ending to the perfect story. Could it have happened any other way? Fans expected Jordan to be superhuman every time out and he never seemed to disappoint. If the saying is true that you're only as good as your last game, then Jordan's legacy is simple: The Greatest.

The legendary curtain-closer.

"He's Michael Jordan—what else can you say? He's a real-life hero."

—Bulls Coach Phil Jackson

IN SI'S WORDS

What has been so amazing is that Jordan has achieved a certain mythology without benefit of our fevered imaginations. Everything he's done is on tape, and has been viewed and reviewed from every angle. None of it has been dreamed or exaggerated. Let the movies depend on special effects, let the politicians rely on spin. Michael Jordan is neomillennial, our first literal legend. And so much of it has been so beautiful. That above all. He made sport into art in a way that we really haven't seen, haven't admired, quite so, since the Greeks chose athletes, foremost, to decorate their amphoras.

In the end, whenever the end, it wasn't so much the basketball. It was the beauty. It truly was a thing of beauty.

—Frank Deford, June 22, 1998

Jazz fans knew what was coming.

Maz's Mash

OCTOBER 13, 1960 To many fans, the Pittsburgh Pirates entered the 1960 World Series as a mere speed-bump on the New York Yankees' road to yet another title. The Pirates had won 95 games during the regular season, but they hadn't won a World Series since 1925 and their lineup was relatively punchless. The mighty Yankees, on the other hand, were playing in their 10th Series in 12 years, and had a lineup studded with superstars like Mickey Mantle, Roger Maris, Yogi Berra and Whitey Ford.

So it came as a surprise that the Series went seven games, and even more so that the score was tied 9–9 in the last of the ninth inning of Game 7. Despite having been pulverized 12–0 in Game 6, and despite scoring only 17 runs to the Yankees 46 during the Series' first six games, the Pirates were still in it.

Second baseman Bill Mazeroski stepped into the batter's box against Ralph Terry. Known more for his glove than his bat, Mazeroski provided the perfect climax to a topsy-turvy Series. He smacked Terry's second pitch over the left-centerfield wall and flew around the bases, arms waving, hat in hand. At home plate he was swarmed by a mob of jubilant teammates. Never before had a World Series ended with a home run. The unlikeliest of heroes had clinched the unlikeliest of victories.

AFTERMATH

Cry not for the Yankees. Sure, they hit .338 as a team in the Series and still lost. Sure, the Series defeat cost Casey Stengel, who had led the Yankees to 10 pennants, his job.

The season may have been cruel by Yankee standards, but they would redeem it the following year. The Bronx Bombers won 109 games in 1961 and advanced to yet another World Series, where they crushed the Cincinnati Reds in five games. Of greater interest, however, was the season-long chase of Babe Ruth's single-season record of 60 home runs. Mantle and Maris both contended, but it was Maris who, after painfully enduring the hounding of an antagonistic press for the most of the year, belted No. 61 on the final day of the season. His record would last for 37 years.

Above and to the right of the clock soars the Yankees' demise.

Miracle in Miami

NOVEMBER 23, 1984 Boston College quarterback Doug Flutie began and ended his passing day against the defending national champion Miami Hurricanes with a toss to Gerard Phelan. The first one got him a five-yard gain to the Miami 21. The last one got him the Heisman Trophy.

Even without the Chip Hilton ending, this would have been one of the great college football games of all time. Flutie and Miami quarterback Bernie Kosar, both of whom would end up in the NFL, played can-you-top-this? all afternoon, combining for 919 passing yards as their teams tossed the lead back and forth like a hot potato.

Miami trailed 41–38 with 3:50 left. Kosar whipped five passses for 80 yards, and running back Melvin Bratton plunged over from the one to drive the Hurricanes back in front, 45–41, with 28 seconds left.

Time enough for Flutie. The winning play, which ranks with the most famous in college football history, can be narrated from memory by highlight-show junkies. Flutie rolls right, stops at his own 37-yard-line, plants his left toe and heaves the ball up into the rainy, windy Miami evening. Sixty-four yards away, the ball whistles down and through the arms of two Miami defensive backs—straight into Phelan's gut as he falls to the end zone turf. Touchdown. Boston College 47, Miami 45.

THE OTHER SIDE

Miami head coach Jimmy Johnson and his defensive coordinator Bill Trout had had their differences before Doug Flutie's Hail Mary was answered, but the famous pass provided the last straw in the two coaches' tempestuous relationship. After the game, Trout announced that he was resigning over "a question of philosophy" with Johnson. Asked of his plans for the future, a frustrated Trout replied that he would enter the "tomato-packing business."

"People don't remember this," Trout told the *Chicago Tribune*, "but in the East Carolina game that year, East Carolina throws the Hail Mary on the final play and [DB Reggie] Sutton did the same thing [bumped a teammate while leaping for the ball]. But the East Carolina receiver juggles the ball and drops it, and we won 12–7. [But] BC made the play....

"Jimmy took that loss like a stake through the heart. What happened happened. I hate to lose, too, but I was proud to have been a part of that game. It was a great game."

Flutie completed 34 passes for 472 yards.

The Natural

OCTOBER 15, 1988 The expression "walk-off home run" was not yet in vogue when the Dodgers' Kirk Gibson hit the winning blast in Game 1 of the 1988 World Series against the A's, and even if it had been, the phrase wouldn't have applied to Gibson's heroics on that memorable night. "Limp-off," maybe, or "hobble-off," but not "walk-off."

Gibson shouldn't have been in uniform, much less at the plate, facing the best closer in baseball, Dennis Eckersley, with two out in the bottom of the ninth and his team trailing 4–3. No, the only Gibson with any business at Dodger Stadium that night was Debbie, who sang the national anthem. Kirk should have been in the trainer's room, icing the hamstring he'd re-strained in Game 5 of the NLCS and the knee he'd injured in Game 7 of that series.

And that's where he had been for the first eight innnings of the game. But when the A's took their one-run lead into the bottom of the ninth and Eckersley came in to pitch, Gibson clambered off the trainer's table and grabbed a bat. Pinch hitter Mike Davis drew a two-out walk, and Gibson limped out of the dugout to the roar of the home crowd. Moments later he delivered his Hollywood ending, punching a full-count slider over the rightfield fence.

Having set the Dodgers on the path to victory, Gibson returned to the trainer's table for the rest of the Series. L.A. knocked off the heavily favored A's in five games.

IN SI'S WORDS

The crowd was on its feet, through three straight foul balls ... and a backdoor slider that barely missed the outside corner; through [Mike] Davis's steal of second ... ; through drama stretched as tight as it could go, to a full count.... In Hollywood, Roy Hobbs hits the ball out to end *The Natural*, but on this night it was Gibson.

Welcome to the California World Series....

He knew what he'd done the instant the ball exploded off his bat. He raised his arm and held it aloft until he reached first base coach Manny Mota. Then he limped around the bases as if he were straggling home from the Russian front, dragging his right leg and stepping gingerly on his left.... While Gibson was mobbed at home plate by fellow Dodgers, bullpen coach Mark Cresse sneaked away and put a sign over the slugger's locker that read ROY HOBBS.

—Peter Gammons, October 24, 1988

Hollywood couldn't have scripted it better.

The Immaculate
Reception

DECEMBER 23, 1972 To each of the 50,350 fans in Pittsburgh's Three Rivers Stadium, it seemed an inescapable fact that the home team was going to lose this AFC semifinal to the Oakland Raiders by a score of 7–6.

The Steelers had the ball, but they were on their own 40-yard line with 22 seconds left. Even Steelers owner Art Rooney had left his seat to go console his players.

At the snap, quarterback Terry Bradshaw rolled right, casting about for a receiver. Franco Harris, the rookie fullback who was supposed to stay in and block on the play, instead ran downfield, thinking that he'd be near the ball and could help whoever it came to. At last Bradshaw spotted Frenchy Fuqua at the Raiders' 35 and whipped a pass in his direction. The football and Raiders defender Jack Tatum hit Fuqua at precisely the same time, and the ball popped up in the air. Out of nowhere Harris appeared, plucked the ball off his shoelaces and rumbled for the winning score.

"Tell them you touched it! Tell them you touched it!" screamed Tatum at Fuqua, desperately invoking a rule, now abolished, that prohibited a player's tapping the ball to a teammate. Fuqua, of course, was mum on the subject. Tatum's protests fell on deaf ears and the touchdown stood. Game over.

AFTERMATH

The football gods must have deemed it overkill to lend the Steelers a helping hand in two consecutive games. Pittsburgh went on to lose the AFC Championship to the Miami Dolphins, 21–17. The Steelers had been blessed by the Immaculate Reception, but the Dolphins were enjoying the Immaculate Season. They would finish at 17–0—a feat unequalled in NFL history—with a 14–7 defeat of Washington in Super Bowl VII.

But the Steelers soon would supplant Miami as the NFL team of the '70s, winning four Super Bowls from the 1974 to '79 seasons, a stretch of six years in which their cumulative regular-season record was 67-20-1. There were countless reasons for the Steelers' success. One was Hall of Famer Harris, who rushed for over 1,000 yards in eight straight seasons. Another was quarterback Terry Bradshaw, twice the Super Bowl MVP. The Steelers also had big-game wide receiver Lynn Swann, and the Steel Curtain defense that included tackle Mean Joe Greene, linebacker Jack Lambert and cornerback Mel Blount, Hall of Famers all. Led by coach Chuck Noll, they had a well-deserved reputation throughout the league: Tough town, even tougher team.

Divine intervention: Harris seemed as surprised as everyone else by his good fortune.

Diego's Dash

JUNE 22, 1986 Left off Argentina's World Cup team as a 17-year-old in 1978, blotted out of the tournament by vicious defenders in '82, Diego Maradona finally got his chance on the world stage in 1986. He did not disappoint, tearing hungrily into the role of World's Best Player as he led Argentina to the title and scored arguably the greatest goal in the history of the tournament along the way.

The goal came in the quarterfinals, against England, and there was already a plaque commemorating it at Mexico City's Azteca Stadium when the final kicked off the following week.

Collecting the ball just beyond midfield, Maradona eluded a pair of defenders with one deft touch and then launched a spectacular 60-yard run to goal. Half Barry Sanders, half Jean-Claude Killy, he slalomed through three England defenders, went around the outrushing goalkeeper, and buried the ball into the empty net as he fell.

It was the crown jewel of Maradona's thoroughly dominating performance in the '86 World Cup. He scored both of Argentina's goals in its 2–0 semifinal victory over Belgium, and when Germany rallied to tie the final at two and seemingly break Argentina's spirit, Maradona delivered a picture-perfect pass to set up the Cup-winning goal—and indelibly stamp his name on the tournament.

IN SI'S WORDS

In this Cup, it appears that a good goalie is the finest asset a team can have. Three of the four quarterfinal games ended in overtime penalty shoot-outs. The shoot-out is hated by all in Mexico City.... The only way to avoid death by penalty kick, it seems, is to have a genius on your side.

Like Diego Maradona, as the 114,580 people who watched him play for Argentina in its 2–1 win over England at Azteca Stadium in Mexico City on Sunday would testify.

The game ... might have ended in a shoot-out had not Maradona intervened with two goals in four minutes, one horrendously tainted, the other perhaps the best of the tournament. On the first, crafty Diegito punched the ball into the net with what looked like a left hook. On the second, he picked up the ball in a crowd just inside midfield and dribbled by four Englishmen, including goalie Peter Shilton, in a broken-field run of more than 55 yards.

—Clive Gammons, June 30, 1986

After Mexico '86, no one doubted that Maradona was the world's best.

Not-So-Great Scott

JANUARY 27, 1991 Super Bowl XXV was played under weirder, more surreal conditions than any of its 24 predecessors, which, when you're talking about the most hyped spectacle in all of sport, is saying something.

Only 10 days earlier, the U.S. had launched Operation Desert Storm in the Persian Gulf. With terrorist retaliation a real possibility, spectators filing into Tampa Stadium had to pass by metal detectors and bomb-sniffing dogs. Despite the sobering prelude, the game quickly grabbed everyone's attention. The New York Giants possessed the ball for a whopping, Super Bowl–record 40:33, but the Bills still led 12–10 at the half and 19–17 late in the fourth quarter. A Matt Bahr field goal gave the Giants a 20–19 lead and set the stage for one of the most intestine-twisting final plays in Super Bowl history.

The Bills drove to the Giants' 29-yard-line with four seconds left, and prepared for a 47-yard field goal attempt to win the game. The kick was makeable, but by no means a cinch. Bills booter Scott Norwood's alltime best was 49 yards. As all Buffalo held its breath, backup quarterback Frank Reich took the snap and spotted the ball for Norwood. The kick went up, drifted toward the right post—and sailed wide. With that, the game ended, and though no one knew it at the time, a heartbreaking streak of futility for the Bills began.

AFTERMATH

As the only team ever to reach four consecutive Super Bowls, the Bills and their fans, surely, have at least one achievement to celebrate. Unfortunately, the Bills lost every one of those four, which ran from 1991 to '94.

Only two other teams, the Minnesota Vikings and the Denver Broncos, have lost four Super Bowls in all, but their defeats were not consecutive; those teams were able to spread their pain over several years and among varied personnel.

Poor Scott Norwood—whose dramatic miss is the one thing everyone remembers about the game—was handed goat's horns for a kick that was never going to be a gimme. After playing in the Bills' 37–24 loss to the Washington Redskins in the following year's Super Bowl, kicking one 21-yard field goal, Norwood was released by Buffalo. Unable to catch on with another team, he retired, but with no feeling of being Fortune's fool. "A lot of people thought my life was ruined, but nothing could be further from the truth," said Norwood seven years after the miss. "Sure, I wish I had made that kick, but my life didn't go into a tailspin."

Norwood's kick started—and stayed—right.

Boston Plea Party

OCTOBER 21, 1975 After 10 heart-stopping innings of heroic performances and reversals of fortune, Cincinnati Reds third baseman Pete Rose stepped into the batter's box in the 11th inning of Game 6 of the 1975 World Series with the score deadlocked 6–6. He paused and turned to Boston catcher Carlton Fisk. "This is some kind of game, isn't it?"

Indeed. Trailing three games to two in the Series, the Red Sox had both squandered a three-run lead and erased a three-run deficit in this back-and-forth affair. Bernie Carbo forged the rally in the bottom of the eighth inning, belting a three-run homer to tie the score at 6. Both teams had opportunities to win after Carbo's clout: Boston loaded the bases with no outs in the ninth but failed to score, and Cincinnati's Joe Morgan saw his potentially game-winning hit snagged by rightfielder Dwight Evans in the top of the 11th.

October 21 had become October 22 by the time Fisk led off the bottom of the 12th. The Boston catcher crushed the second pitch he saw toward the Green Monster in leftfield, but the ball was hooking foul. Fisk hopped anxiously down the first base line, waving his arms toward fair territory as if he could will the ball to stay in play. When it caromed off the foul pole for a home run, Fisk broke into a sprint around the bases—amidst a sea of half-crazed fans—to score the winning run.

AFTERMATH

Boston may have won the battle, but Cincinnati won the war. Carlton Fisk's heroics were so memorable they make it easy to forget that the Reds—the Big Red Machine, as they were known—rebounded from the dramatic Game 6 loss to win their first World Series in 35 years the next night. Game 7 was almost as exciting as the previous night's tilt. Once again, the Sox jumped out to a 3–0 lead, but Cincinnati first baseman Tony Perez smacked a two-run homer in the sixth inning, and the Reds scored a run to tie the game in the seventh. Joe Morgan hit a run-scoring bloop single in the top of the ninth, and reliever Will McEnaney pitched a 1-2-3 bottom half to seal the win.

In all, there were five one-run games in the Series, which also included two extra-inning affairs and two more that were decided in the ninth inning. "I don't know that there's ever been a better World Series," said Cincinnati manager Sparky Anderson after Game 7. Twenty-five years later, his words still ring true.

Fisk's 12th-inning blast was nearly a foul ball.

The Greatest Game Ever

DECEMBER 28, 1958 NFL commissioner Bert Bell called it "the greatest game I've ever seen," and no wonder. The 1958 NFL title game between the New York Giants and the Baltimore Colts at Yankee Stadium featured 15 future Hall of Famers, including Johnny Unitas, Raymond Berry, Sam Huff and Frank Gifford. But the unexpected star was Charlie Conerly, the Giants' 37-year-old backup quarterback, who rallied his team from a 14–3 deficit to a 17–14 lead. The Colts tied it with seven seconds left in regulation.

This was a game that had everything, including controversy. In a fourth quarter pileup, Colts end Gino Marchetti snapped the two bones in his right leg so loudly it sounded like a gunshot. In the ensuing confusion, the referee may have cost the Giants a critical first down with a poor spot of the ball. The Giants certainly thought so.

In overtime, Unitas engineered a brilliant 80-yard drive that ended with a hand-off to Alan Ameche, who crashed over right tackle for the winning score as fans stormed the field.

Colts coach Weeb Ewbank gave Marchetti the game ball. "Hell," said Marchetti, "I oughta cut this thing up into 50 pieces. I never saw a game that had so much. So many players who made such big plays."

IN SI'S WORDS

Never has there been a game like this one. When there are so many high points, it is not easy to pick the highest. But for the 60,000 and more fans who packed Yankee Stadium last Sunday ... the moment they will never forget — the moment with which they will eternally bore their grandchildren — came when, with less than 10 seconds to play and the clock remorselessly moving, the Baltimore Colts kicked a field goal which put the professional football championship in a 17–17 tie and necessitated a historic sudden-death overtime period. Although it was far from apparent at the time, this was the end of the line for the fabulous New York Giants, eastern titleholders by virtue of three stunning victories over a great Cleveland team ... and the heroes of one of the most courageous comebacks in the memory of the oldest fans.

—Tex Maule, January 5, 1959

Ameche's plunge ended the first overtime title game in the NFL's 38-year history.

Joe Cool

JANUARY 22, 1989 It's been noted dozens of times before, but it bears repeating: At the start of the 49ers' pressure-packed drive for the winning score in Super Bowl XXIII, with the crowd roaring and the clock ticking down and his team on its own eight-yard-line, trailing by three, Joe Montana tapped one of his linemen on the shoulder pad and pointed to the first row of Miami's Joe Robbie Stadium. "Hey, look over there," he said. "There's John Candy."

The Montana legend was already well stocked with thrilling comebacks, with The Catch, with two Super Bowl rings and two Super Bowl MVP awards. Maybe that's why he was calm enough to engage in a little celebrity spotting amid the frenzy.

More likely, though, it was just Joe Cool being himself, hardwired for grace under pressure, as he had been his entire career. San Francisco trailed 16–13 with 3:20 to play. The 92 yards between the 49ers and victory didn't seemed to bother Joe. Quite the opposite, in fact. He was about to complete seven precision passes, call a timeout, then zip the ball 10 yards over the middle to John Taylor for the winning score with 34 seconds left. No problem. But first, let's pause to note the comedian in the crowd.

Just another chapter in the storied Montana legend.

THE OTHER SIDE

Even before they lost to the 49ers in Super Bowl XXIII, the Bengals had had a rough week. First, Overtown, the Miami neighborhood in which the team had booked hotel rooms, erupted in riots after a shooting by the police. Then fullback Stanley Wilson missed a team meeting and was found high on cocaine in his room. Then All-Pro lineman Tim Krumrie went down with a broken leg on the second possession of the game.

Lastly, of course, there was Montana to vex them. When the Niners took over on their own eight-yard-line in the waning minutes, a Cincinnati teammate told Cris Collinsworth on the sidelines, "We got them now." Collinsworth remembered asking the fellow if he knew about No. 16 for the Niners. "That's what it came down to," he said. "Joe Montana is not human. I don't want to call him a god, but he's definitely somewhere in between."

"We were only 34 seconds away," said Bengals coach Sam Wyche when the comeback was complete. "Just 34."

With Montana at the controls, San Francisco's game-winning drive seemed inevitable.

"Havlicek Stole the Ball!"

APRIL 15, 1965 The Boston Celtics had run their streak of NBA titles to six by 1965, and their fans, including the gravel-voiced radio broadcaster Johnny Most, seemed to believe that the streak could go on forever. So it was shocking to find the Celtics in danger of being eliminated by the Philadelphia 76ers, upstarts who had made themselves instantly stronger by re-acquiring Wilt Chamberlain in a midseason trade with the San Francisco Warriors. With five seconds to play in a ragged game, the Celtics had the lead, 110–109, but the Sixers had the ball. Boston fans stood four and five deep behind the Sixers' Hal Greer as he prepared to inbound the ball from under the Boston basket.

John Havlicek, Boston's scrappy 6'5" forward, anticipated the pass and raced back toward mid-court, where Philadelphia's Chet Walker was awaiting the ball. Havlicek leaped and with his right hand tipped the ball to his teammate, Sam Jones, who dribbled the five seconds off the clock. Most's famous, froggy-voiced call became legendary: "Havlicek stole the ball! ... Havlicek stole the ball!"

The Celtics went on to beat the Lakers in the finals for the seventh title in their string of eight, the longest streak in the history of professional team sports.

SPOTLIGHT

In his 37 years behind the microphone at Boston Garden, Johnny Most never aimed for objectivity. He was the ultimate Celtics fan and made no apologies for it. In a voice gnarled by his four-packs-a-day smoking habit—English Oval was his brand—Most called games as if his beloved Celtics were the last bastion of moral rectitude in a world gone to seed. While Boston stars like Havlicek—who averaged 20.8 points a game in his 16-year Hall of Fame career—could do no wrong, opponents were rebuked for their shortcomings. Most once accused the Warrior's Rick Barry of "crying again, the big baby."

When Most died of a heart attack in 1993, Boston fans turned out for his memorial en masse. "He gave us permission to take the game seriously," said Most's eulogist, rabbi Harry Kushner. "He turned it into a morality play."

The camera caught the precise instant that Most immortalized.

The Putt Heard 'Round The World

SEPTEMBER 26, 1999 As Saturday turned into Sunday at the Country Club in Brookline, Mass., Europe stood poised to win its third consecutive Ryder Cup. In 32 previous Cups, no team had ever rallied from more than two points down. The Americans would start Sunday trailing by four. To regain the Cup, they would have to win eight of the 12 matches that day, and tie one.

For a team that included six of the Top 10 players in the World Ranking, a comeback wasn't *impossible*, just totally, utterly unlikely. But the U.S. staged a miraculous charge to seize a 14–11 lead with three matches to play. Half a point more and the Cup would be theirs.

Enter Justin Leonard. Tied with José María Olazábal at 17, Leonard, if he won the hole, would go one up with one hole to play, thereby clinching the crucial half point for the U.S. But with both men facing long birdie putts—Leonard's was 45 feet, Olazábal's 20—it seemed the matter would not be settled until 18.

Leonard rolled his putt toward the cup, and the onlooking U.S. team exploded when it disappeared: a bolt from the blue that sealed one of the greatest comebacks in golf history. Or almost. Olazábal had yet to putt, so the U.S. celebration was not only premature, it was also unseemly. If Olazábal made his putt, Europe would still have a chance. He took his time, lined up his shot—and missed. Now the celebration could begin.

IN SI'S WORDS

[U.S. captain Ben] Crenshaw hugged Leonard so hard that it looked as if his piercing blue eyes might pop right out of his head....

[Crenshaw, an avid student of golf's history,] would collect his cup and his memories and himself. Crenshaw first came to the Country Club in 1968, to play in the U.S. Junior Amateur. His father, Charlie, who died this past May, was at that championship, walking the fairways of the Country Club with his 16-year-old boy. Young Ben fell for the game in a way few people can understand. His first marriage could not withstand his love for the game. His second one is guided by it.

"We gave up our lives for this," Crenshaw said. "We gave up our kids. I gave up my golf for this. I don't even play golf anymore."

Was it worth it?

His weeping told you all you needed to know. The historian had made history.

—Michael Bamberger, October 4, 1999

Leonard's astounding 45-footer redeemed what had been a poor Cup for him.

Headlong into History

MAY 10, 1970 Bruins center Derek Sanderson made the pass that led to Bobby Orr's famous goal in the 1970 Stanley Cup, but the assist on the moment's leap into legend goes to photographer Ray Lussier. Lussier's shutter caught Orr in mid-flight, parallel to the ice, after he had beaten St. Louis goaltender Glenn Hall and been clipped by defenseman Noel Picard. Orr's stick is already raised in celebration, and his face is lit up with the knowledge that he has just delivered the Bruins their first championship since 1941. The goal, which gave Boston a 4–3 sudden-death overtime victory and a sweep of the Cup, was certainly dramatic; Lussier's spectacular photograph made it immortal.

Not that Orr, who revolutionized the defenseman's role with his electrifying, rink-length rushes, needed help from timely photography to secure membership in the NHL pantheon. His Cup-winning goal was the crowning glory to an astonishing season in which he became the first defenseman ever to lead the league in scoring (120 points), won the Hart Trophy as the league's most valuable player, and was named *Sports Illustrated*'s Sportsman of the Year. The Hall of Fame would follow, and in 1996, the NHL selected his unforgettable goal as the greatest moment in its 79-year history.

AFTERMATH

Orr trumped his superb 1970 season the following year by racking up 139 points, including an NHL-record 102 assists. He would have led the league in scoring again if his teammate Phil Esposito hadn't exploded for 76 goals and 152 points, both records. Indeed, the '71 Bruins enjoyed one of the greatest regular seasons ever, winning an unprecedented 57 games. Esposito, Orr, John Bucyk and Ken Hodge finished 1-2-3-4 in the league scoring race, and Orr won a second straight Hart Trophy as well as a fourth consecutive Norris Trophy as the league's top defenseman (he would win eight in a row in his career). But it all came crashing down in the quarterfinals of the playoffs when Boston ran into Montreal and its red-hot goaltender, Ken Dryden. The Canadiens upset the Bruins in seven games.

Undeterred, Orr and the Bruins returned to the Stanley Cup finals in '72 and defeated the New York Rangers—thanks to Orr's series-clinching goal in Game 6.

Orr soared into NHL lore.

Carter's Clout

OCTOBER 23, 1993 Despite losing eight players from the previous year's team, the defending champion Toronto Blue Jays had won 95 games in 1993, captured the AL East by seven games over the Yankees and dispatched the White Sox in six for the American League pennant. They were the clear favorite in the World Series against the upstart Philadelphia Phillies.

Toronto's only weakness was pitching, a fact confirmed in Game 4 of this seesaw Series, a 15–14 slugfest played in a steady drizzle at Philadelphia's veteran stadium. The game set Series records for duration (4:14), runs scored (29) and runs scored by a losing team (14). Toronto pitching had surrendered 14 runs, yes, but the Blue Jays had won, thanks to a six-run eighth inning against Philadelphia reliever Mitch (Wild Thing) Williams.

The high-scoring victory gave the Blue Jays a commanding 3–1 Series lead, but Philadelphia ace Curt Schilling hurled a complete-game gem in Game 5, which the Phils won 2–0 to send the series back to Toronto.

The star for the Blue Jays so far had been future Hall of Famer Paul Molitor who, in 15 previous seasons, had never played for a

Carter watched the ball leave the park (left), then set off deliriously around the bases.

"I can't even describe the feeling. I don't think they've made that word up yet. I still can't believe it happened."

—Joe Carter

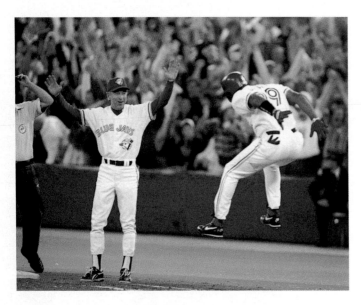

THE OTHER SIDE

The Philadelphia Phillies were not supposed to be in this World Series, facing the defending champion Toronto Blue Jays. They were a ragtag army of headcases and misfits anchored by reliever Mitch Williams, who was known as Wild Thing. "You can't get on this club wihout a letter from a psychiatrist," said star pitcher Curt Schilling.

It had been eight seasons since the Phillies topped .500, yet in 1993 they jumped out to a huge midseason lead and improbably held onto it. Then they further shocked everyone by beating Atlanta in the NLCS.

When Williams came in to pitch the ninth inning in Game 6 of the Series, he had already suffered through a disastrous outing in Game 4. Now, with his team's survival at stake, he walked Rickey Henderson, got an out, and gave up a single to Paul Molitor. Then Joe Carter came to bat. A month and a half later, the Phillies, citing the vitriolic fan reaction to his Series performance, traded Williams to Houston. He stumbled to a 1–4 start with a 7.65 ERA, and was released in May '94. Williams attempted a brief comeback in '95, appearing in 20 games for the Anaheim Angels and going 1–2 with a 6.75 ERA. He has been out of baseball ever since.

champion. He batted .500 and was named MVP of the Series.

Blue Jays rightfielder Joe Carter had also been productive, with one home run and four RBIs to his name as Game 6 began. Toronto had blown a 5–1 lead in the game, and trailed 6–5 in the bottom of the ninth. With two on and one out, Carter worked a 2–2 count against Williams, then drilled a low, inside pitch over the leftfield fence. It was the first time a team had rallied to win the World Series with a homer. Carter bounded in delirious joy around the bases, and Molitor, a champion at last, ran around hugging his teammates and weeping.

Make way for the hero: After his joyous basepath romp (above) Carter planted his foot on home plate.

Legendmakers

Introduction

Jim Thorpe (left) made his legend at the 1912 Olympics.

It is Malvolio, the pompous and puritanical steward in Shakespeare's *Twelfth Night*, who has catalogued most memorably the different paths to greatness: "Some men are born great," he said, "some achieve greatness, and some have greatness thrust upon them."

The magical kingdom of Illyria is a long way from the glitzy, hard-nosed world of modern sports, but for the 15 moments in our Legendmakers chapter, Malvolio's list still applies. With one important difference: To achieve their legend-making moments, our athletes followed not one but usually all three of Malvolio's paths. All were born great, possessed of physical talent of an order we might well describe as genius. How else are we to explain the great Brazilian soccer star Pelé, just 17 years old and, amazingly, unawed by the grandest tournament in all of sports, scoring two goals against Sweden in the 1958 World Cup final? Or the versatile Babe Didrikson's sudden rise from near anonymity in Beaumont, Texas, to worldwide fame in the Olympics? Or Secretariat, who ran away from the field to win the Belmont Stakes by an unheard-of 31 lengths. Theirs is physical genius of a cosmically different order.

And after being born with enormous gifts, our legends worked hard to develop their talent. Perhaps Babe Ruth, whose love of beer, hot dogs and late nights often seemed calculated to erode his talents rather than develop them, is something of an exception here, but

The achievements of Carl Lewis (right) in 1984, and Heiden (below) in 1980, will not be soon forgotten.

think of Eric Heiden, whose endless hours in the weight room and on the ice honed his innate talent. In 1980, he vaulted into legend with what is surely the most amazing sweep in Olympic history, winning gold medals in all five men's speed skating events at the Winter Olympics.

Then there's Wilma Rudolph, whose courage and industry enabled her to overcome childhood illnesses which some thought would mean she'd never again walk properly. Or the monumentally tough Joe Frazier, who may not have won the Thrilla in Manila, but who became a fabled fighter because of his game perfromance in the epic bout. "Don't worry son," said cornerman Eddie Futch. "No one will ever forget what you did here today."

The same could be said about all of our legend-making moments. They are unforgettable not only for their inherent greatness but also because they took place on the grandest of stages: The Olympics, the World Cup, the Super

Bowl or World Series. Many were the crowning moments of long and glorious careers. John Elway didn't really need to win Super Bowl XXXII to prove what a great quarterback he was, any more than Reggie Jackson needed his three home runs in Game 6 of the 1977 World Series to show us what a great clutch hitter he was. Those flourishes are exclamation points on already superb careers. One exception is Bobby Thomson's legendary moment, The Shot Heard Round the World. His 1951 pennant-winning homer was the indisputable highlight of the .270 hitter's career.

Yet like all of the athletes on the following pages, Thomson was born with talent, worked hard to develop it, and made the most of the chance for greatness that was thrust upon him.

The Thrilla in Manila

OCTOBER 1, 1975 Muhammad Ali found the perfect foil in Joe Frazier. Ali was a tall, handsome man blessed with speed, grace and a mouth that would not stop. "I am the greatest! I am the prettiest!" he proclaimed, and many resented his braggadocio, but few could dispute his claims. Frazier, on the other hand, was a stolid, stocky brawler—Ali's polar opposite in and out of the ring.

The Thrilla in Manila was the third meeting between the two. Frazier had won the first, a 15-rounder in New York in 1971, but Ali came back three years later to beat him, and by 1975, most ring fans considered Frazier a has-been. In 1973, he had been pummeled by George Foreman, whom Ali had knocked out in eight rounds.

This fight, however, showed something else. After 10 brutal, back-and-forth rounds, the bout was even. Frazier spent his remaining

"I thought you were washed up."

—Muhammad Ali, to Joe Frazier

Ali (above right, and left, in white trunks) staged a furious assault in Rounds 13 and 14.

"No one will ever forget what you did here today."

—Frazier's manager Eddie Futch

IN SI'S WORDS

Ali's version of death began about 10:45 a.m. on Oct. 1 in Manila. Up to then his attitude had been almost frivolous. He would simply not accept Joe Frazier as a man or as a fighter, despite the bitter lesson Frazier had given him in their first savage meeting. Esthetics govern all of Ali's actions and conclusions; the way a man looks, the way he moves is what interests Ali. By Ali's standards, Frazier was not pretty as a man and without semblance of style as a fighter. Frazier was an affront to beauty, to Ali's own beauty as well as to his precious concept of how a good fighter should move. Ali did not hate Frazier, but he viewed him with the contempt of a man who cannot bear anything short of physical and professional perfection.

—Mark Kram, October 13, 1975

energy in a furious 11th-round onslaught that left Ali's corner in awe. "Lord have mercy!" prayed trainer Bundini Brown. Ali found one last store of resolve. He knocked Frazier's mouthpiece into press row in the 13th, and after 14 Frazier's trainer threw in the towel.

"Man, I hit him with punches that'd bring down the walls of a city," Frazier said later. Even Ali was in awe of the thing he and Frazier had shared. "It was like death," he said. "Closest thing to dyin' that I know of."

Despite losing the bout, Frazier (above, and right, in blue trunks) came out a hero.

A-Mays-ing

SEPTEMBER 29, 1954 The Cleveland Indians of 1954 were a fearsome bunch. With three future Hall of Fame pitchers (Bob Lemon, Hal Newhouser and Early Wynn) and the potent bats of Larry Doby and Vic Wertz, the Indians had won an AL-record 111 games. They were heavy favorites to whip the New York Giants in the '54 World Series.

None of that aura of invincibility disappeared when, in the first inning of Game 1, Wertz tripled off Sal Maglie to give the Indians a 2–0 lead. The Giants came back to tie the game in the bottom of the third, and the score was still 2–2 in the top of the eighth when Wertz came to bat against Don Liddle. There were two men on and no outs. Wertz drove a ball to deepest centerfield, a ball that would have been a home run in Cleveland—or any other ballpark, for that matter. Mays turned and set off in pursuit. He caught up to the ball about 450 feet from home plate and pulled it in over his shoulder while running full speed. It was, in the estimation of everyone but those who watched him play day in and day out, the greatest catch ever. "It was a helluva catch," conceded Giant pitcher Johnny Antonelli, "yet it was just a typical Willie Mays play. His throw back to the infield as he fell down, preventing them from scoring, was just as good."

AFTERMATH

Mays's improbable catch seemed to break Cleveland's spirit. Or the spirit of all the Indians but Wertz, who had an exceptional Series, going eight for 16 with two doubles, a triple and a home run. Wertz doubled in the 10th inning of Game 1 but his teammates couldn't get him home, and the Giants scored three runs in the bottom of the inning to win. New York went on to sweep the supposedly invincible Indians with three straight, somewhat anticlimactic, victories.

Mays, of course, went on to have arguably the greatest career in the history of professional baseball. Along with his routinely amazing exploits in centerfield, he blended speed and power as few players before or after him have. Mays retired in 1973 with a lifetime average of .302 and 660 career homers, third on the alltime list behind Hank Aaron and Babe Ruth. He was the first man to hit 300 homers and steal 300 bases, and he scored at least 100 runs in 12 straight seasons.

"I had that one all the way," Mays told teammate Monte Irvin.

Where There's a Will, There's Elway

JANUARY 25, 1998 Sometimes one game, or even one play, can change a player's entire career. John Elway was already a great quarterback before Super Bowl XXXII. He had passed for 48,669 yards in his career, and was legendary for delivering in the clutch. His ticket to Canton had already been punched. But to many—truth be told—he retained the aura of loser. Three times he had led Denver to the Super Bowl, and three times the Broncos had been humiliated.

In Supe XXXII, though, the Broncos believed they could beat the Green Bay Packers. With the score tied late in the third quarter, Elway laid the ghosts of Super Bowls past to rest with one gutty play. Finding his receivers covered on a third-and-six at the Green Bay 12, he tucked the ball under his arm and took off. This wasn't the fleet Elway of old. This was a 37-year-old veteran of six knee surgeries. As Packers safety LeRoy Butler closed in, Elway launched his body into the air. The two collided and Elway went spinning like a top, but when he landed, he had the first down. Two plays later Denver scored. They would go on to upset the Packers 31–24.

Elway's courageous leap had redoubled his team's determination and proved, again and indisputably, that he was a champion.

IN SI'S WORDS

When Elway hit the ground at the four, an adrenaline rush surged through the Broncos. Denver scored two plays later, and though the Packers came back to tie the score again, Green Bay was a depleted team fighting a losing battle against an opponent that had been recharged. When the Broncos launched their game-winning drive from the Packers' 49 with 3:27 remaining, it was like watching a battle of the bands between Pearl Jam and the Kingston Trio. "When Elway, instead of running out of bounds, turned it up and got spun around like a helicopter, it energized us beyond belief," Denver defensive lineman Mike Lodish said after the game. Added Shannon Sharpe, the Broncos' All-Pro tight end, "When I saw him do that and then get up pumping his fist, I said, 'It's on.' That's when I was sure we were going to win."

—Michael Silver, February 2, 1998

Denver fans now have the Run to cherish along with the Drive.

Total Babe

AUGUST 4, 1932 Mildred (Babe) Didrikson was way ahead of her time, and not only as a groundbreaking female athlete. She may well have been the first trash-talking star. Didrikson perfected Muhammad Ali's schtick before Muhammad Ali was born. Prior to golf tournaments, she used to ask her opponents who was playing for second; and often, after crushing a drive out over the fairway, she would turn to the gallery and say, "Boy! Don't you wish men could hit a ball like that?"

Her incessant bragging rubbed some—make that most—of her competitors the wrong way, but like Ali three decades later, Didrikson could back it up. En route to the 1932 Olympic Games in Los Angeles, she shouted to a crowd in Albuquerque, "Ever heard of Babe Didrikson? You will! You will!" Then she won the javelin with an Olympic-record toss and destroyed the world record in the 80-meter hurdles for her second gold, and all of America *had* heard of her. Didrikson broke the world record in her next event, the high jump, but had to settle for silver on a technicality.

The '32 Games were unequivocally hers. When they were over, her fame approached that of the other Babe—Babe Ruth—and she moved on to her next challenge: becoming the best woman golfer in the world.

SPOTLIGHT

Dubbed 'Babe' by the boys on the sandlots of Beaumont, Texas, because of the Ruthian fly balls she uncorked in baseball, Mildred Didrikson excelled at every sport she tried, and she tried them all. In 1932, she entered the AAU nationals in track and field—and won. The entire meet. Single-handedly. That's right, Didrikson's point total—she took first in six of the eight events she entered, and set three world records—was eight points better than the second-place *team*. Which consisted of 22 women.

Like her namesake in the Bronx, Didrikson attracted, and embellished, tall tales about her exploits, but that one is true. And so are these: Didrikson won a record 17 straight golf tournaments in 1946 and '47, and in 1954, only 15 months after surgery for the cancer that would take her life two years later, Didrikson won the U.S. Women's Open by 12 strokes. Swagger, a taste for high living, and athletic superiority, Didrikson had all these in common with Babe Ruth—and this too: there will never be another one like her.

Didrikson (far right) broke the world record in the 80-meter hurdles.

Golden Boy

FEBRUARY 23 1980 The 1980 U.S. Olympic hockey team's spectacular upset of the Soviets has had a longer life in the American popular imagination, but speed skater Eric Heiden's accomplishments at Lake Placid, which shared the headlines with the hockey team at the time, are hardly less remarkable. And considering how the sport has become specialized, they are unlikely ever to be approached, much less equaled.

A 21-year-old from Madison, Wisc., with a an easy smile and cannon-barrel thighs, Heiden became the first athlete in Olympic history to win five individual gold medals at a single Games. Astoundingly versatile, he won gold in events from 500 meters to 10,000. Imagine U.S. sprinter Michael Johnson winning the 400-meter dash *and* the 10K. Not to mention every event in between. Heiden took the 500 in an Olympic-record 38.03 seconds, and the 10,000 in a world-record 14:28.13. He set Olympic records in his other three events, the 1,000, 1,500 and 5,000. "In Norway," said coach Sten Stenson, "we say that if you can be good in the 5,000 and 10,000, you cannot do the 500. But Eric can do it. We have no idea how to train to take him. We just hope he retires."

His place in the Olympic pantheon secure, Heiden gave Stenson his wish after Lake Placid.

AFTERMATH

Turning down several lucrative endorsement and film offers, Eric Heiden enrolled at Stanford University as a premed student following the 1980 Olympics. "Ever since I was a little kid, I wanted to be a doctor," he said. After a brief stint as a cyclist, during which he won a U.S. professional title (in 1985), and competed in the Tour de France (in '86), Heiden graduated from medical school in May 1991. Following in his father's footsteps, he became an orthopedic surgeon.

In 1999 Heiden had an orthopedics practice at the University of California at Davis, with a sideline as the team doctor for the Sacramento Kings of the NBA. In December of that year he returned to the ice—as the doctor for the U.S. team at the world junior hockey championships in Skelleftea, Sweden. Most of Heiden's charges knew little or nothing of his legendary exploits at Lake Placid, and that's the way the Doc wanted it.

Heiden skated to a clean sweep at Lake Placid.

GREATEST MOMENTS

The Miracle of Coogan's Bluff

OCTOBER 3, 1951 The New York Giants trailed the Brooklyn Dodgers by 13½ games in August of 1951. Brooklyn had its best team in years and could already taste the championship. The taste got fainter, though, as the Giants embarked on a late-season tear, winning 37 of their last 44 games to tie Brooklyn at the end of the year, forcing a three-game playoff for the National League pennant. The teams split the first two games, and the entire season came down to one game at the Polo Grounds, on Coogan's Bluff in upper Manhattan.

Brooklyn's ace Don Newcombe handcuffed the Giants for eight innings and held a 4–1 lead in the bottom of the ninth inning. The Dodgers needed only three outs to advance to the World Series. But a pair of singles and a Whitey Lockman double made the score 4–2, and prompted Brooklyn manager Charlie Dressen to summon Ralph Branca— No. 13—to face Bobby Thomson. Thomson had hit a home run off Branca in the first game of the playoff. The Dodgers could have walked him to get to a rookie named Willie Mays, but decided not to. Bad decision. Thomson smacked Branca's second pitch into the leftfield stands for a three-run home run. The Giants had won the pennant, as Russ Hodges famously confirmed over and over again to his radio audience, and Brooklyn fans were left muttering their annual refrain, "Wait till next year."

Thomson's immortal shot soared over leftfielder Andy Pafko and into the seats.

"The Giants win the pennant! The Giants win the pennant!"

—Russ Hodges, radio announcer

THE OTHER SIDE

Bobby Thomson. Ralph Branca. There is no one without the other. One man belted the "Shot Heard 'Round the World." The other has spent a lifetime answering questions about serving it up.

Branca was only 25 years old when Thomson made him famous. But he had been in the majors long enough to start an All-Star game (1948), top 20 wins in a season (21 in 1947) and win a World Series game (he beat the Yankees in 1947). He won 13 games and pitched over 200 innings for Dem Bums in 1951, but most people only remember his last pitch of that season. "I realized that I had done the best I could," Branca said later. "The guy just hit a home run. He was better than I was this day. Life goes on."

Sadly, Branca never recaptured his 20-win form. Injuries limited him to only 12 more wins in five more seasons, and by age 30, he was out of baseball.

Thomson's teammates mobbed him at home plate.

Battle of the Sexes

SEPTEMBER 20, 1973 It was a rivalry as old as Cain-versus-Abel and as bitter as Yankees-versus-Red Sox. It was Man-versus-Woman, in the form of a tennis match between Big-Mouth Chauvinist Bobby Riggs and Feminist Champion Billie Jean King. The prospect of seeing the two battle for $100,000 was enough to lure more than 30,000 spectators to the Houston Astrodome.

Of course, the whole thing was absurd. King was 29 and the reigning Wimbledon women's champion, while Riggs, though undeniably a man, was 55 years old, and well past his prime. "He's an old man, he walks like a duck, he can't see … and, besides, he's an idiot," said King's pal Rosie Casals.

In the end, King whipped Riggs, 6–4, 6–3, 6–3, employing, ironically, what most people thought of as the "man's" game of serve-and-volley. She attacked his first serves, ran him ragged around the baseline and so exhausted Riggs that by the third set his racquet hand cramped. "I didn't know Billie Jean was so quick," confessed Riggs.

What in the world did it prove? According to the *New York Times*, King's triumph "convinced skeptics that a female athlete can survive pressure-filled situations and that men are as susceptible to nerves as women." It's hard to believe there was ever a time when we needed to be convinced of that. We've all come a long way, baby.

IN SI'S WORDS

At this point in time it is perfectly clear that what this country needs is a tennis match between a baboon and a cucumber. We have handled man vs. woman now, twice, with considerable grace and style. It is time to move on to the biggies.

For example, as accompaniment to Billie Jean King and Bobby Riggs right there on the floor of the Astrodome, America's Indoor Taste City, the temptation must have been to avoid decency and present us with all manner of tacky stuff: dwarfs singing at the champagne bar, Liberace riding in a Naugahyde Skylab.

But no. All Promoter Jerry Perenchio displayed in front of 30,472 people live, and a few dozen more watching around the world, was King–Riggs straight up, Riggs–King unadorned; Billie Jean against Robert Larimore for $100,000, winner take all.

Of course, there were the obligatory band musicians by the hundreds, dancing girls by the thousands; hardhats and hippies, libbers and lobbers, chauvinists and charlatans ....

—Curry Kirkpatrick, October 1, 1973

King chuckled at the cartoonish pageantry attending the match.

The Boy Who Would Be King

JUNE 29, 1958 No one outside of Brazil had ever heard of him, a 17-year-old boy fresh from his first professional season with the São Paulo club Santos. And until the moment he boarded the plane to Sweden for the 1958 World Cup, Pelé feared they might not get the chance. He had injured his knee a few weeks earlier, and with the wealth of talent available in his country, Pelé was sure that he would be dropped in favor of a fit player.

But Brazil's coach, Vicente Feola, knew he had something special in the precocious striker, and decided to keep him. Pelé made his debut in Brazil's third game, against Russia, one of the favorites. The youngest player ever to appear in the World Cup set up the second goal in a convincing 2–0 victory.

In a hard-fought quarterfinal against Wales, Pelé scored the only goal of the game. Against France in the semis, he scored a hat-trick. The final, against Sweden, was almost a formality, so confident were the Brazilians. After conceding an early goal, they dismantled the Swedes with a sparkling display of teamwork and individualism. Pelé scored to start the second half, then put an exclamation on the triumph just before the final whistle, heading home his sixth goal of the Cup to give Brazil a 5–2 victory. Now the entire world knew his name.

AFTERMATH

Pelé may have been Brazil's secret weapon as a little-known 17-year-old in 1958, but by the time the 1962 World Cup began in Chile, he was widely acknowledged as the greatest player in the world. Unfortunately, a pulled hamstring in Brazil's second game at Chile '62 forced him out of the tournament. But Brazil, demonstrating the vast depth of its soccer talent, won the Cup without him. Pelé returned in 1966, when England hosted the tournament, only to be savaged by defenders and left unprotected by referees. He sat out Brazil's second game, a 3–1 loss to Hungary, because of the battering he took in its first, a 2–0 win over Bulgaria. After Brazil was eliminated by Portugal in its next game, a bruised and bitter Pelé vowed he would never play in the World Cup again. Happily, he didn't stick to his vow, returning in 1970 to lead Brazil to an unprecedented third world championship.

If Pelé (left, and above right, scoring against Sweden) was overawed by the occasion, he didn't show it.

Decking der Führer

JUNE 22, 1938 "He's a credit to his race," was the backhanded compliment white America paid to Joe Louis after he captured the heavyweight title in 1937. But on the eve of Louis's title defense against Germany's Max Schmeling, America suddenly recast him as a patriot—a defender of American ideals against those of Adolf Hitler's Nazi Germany. Schmeling was the reluctant villain in what the press dubbed a match of good versus evil.

Though he had suffered his only professional defeat to Schmeling two years earlier, Louis planned to be the aggressor in their rematch. Thirty seconds into the fight he swung a sledgehammer right cross into Schmeling's left side that fractured a bone in his vertebrae. "I guess maybe it was a lucky punch," Louis said, "but man, did he scream!"

Schmeling could barely raise his left arm, and Louis moved in to finish him. A right to the jaw floored Schmeling, but the German regained his feet at the count of three. Another right dropped him again, but Schmeling, dazed and acting on instinct, bounced up quickly once more. A final right from Louis ended the beating.

The fight lasted only 2:04 but the respect and admiration it earned Louis were eternal. As columnist Jimmy Cannon later wrote: "He's a credit to his race—the human race."

IN SI'S WORDS

At 9 p.m. trainer Jack Blackburn woke Louis to tape his hands. It was a familiar, soothing ritual. Usually Louis shadowboxed for 10 minutes before a fight. But tonight he did it for half an hour. He wanted to be ready to spring to the attack at the opening bell. Then the champion was escorted to the ring in a circle of uniformed policemen. In his dressing room Schmeling listened to the crowd roar for Louis. Then he headed to the ring, encircled by a tense police escort. The crowd in the stands applauded the German, but fans on the infield hurled banana peels and paper cups at him. Schmeling covered his head with a towel. In the moments before the bell, Louis danced and punched the air. Sweat gleamed on his skin. Schmeling stood motionless, arms hanging at his sides. He stared at Louis. The bell rang and Max Schmeling walked out quickly to meet Joe Louis.

—Chris Mead, September 23, 1985

Louis (striped trunks) dropped Schmeling three times in two minutes.

OCTOBER 18, 1977 "If I played in New York," said Reggie Jackson in 1972, when he was with the Oakland A's, "they would name a candy bar after me."

Hitting, not humility, was Jackson's forte, and as a clutch batter, he had few peers. He got the chance to test his swagger in 1977, after the Yankees acquired his services for five years and $2.9 million. The deal turned out to be a bargain for New York as Jackson batted .286 with 32 home runs and 110 RBIs to lead the Yanks to the World Series, where he earned his nickname, Mr. October.

"Reggie! Reggie! Reggie!"

Jackson thrived in the postseason.

"I'm the straw
that stirs the drink."

—Reggie Jackson

The scene was Yankee Stadium, Game 6. Facing elimination if they lost, the Los Angeles Dodgers held a 3–2 lead in the fourth inning when Jackson came to the plate with a man on. He sent Burt Hooton's first pitch over the right centerfield fence to put the Yanks back in front. At bat again in the fifth inning, with one runner on and the Yankees leading 5–3, Jackson effectively ended the game by taking the first pitch from Elias Sosa and parking it to rightfield. New York 7, LA 3. That was the score when Jackson stepped into the batter's box to face knuckleballer Charlie Hough in the eighth. Hough's first offering fluttered in. Jackson waited—and creamed the ball to straightaway centerfield. Not since Babe Ruth in 1928 had anyone bashed three home runs in a World Series game. Reggie Bars would hit candy store shelves nationwide in 1980.

AFTERMATH

Reggie Jackson finished the 1977 World Series with five home runs, a .450 batting average and the landslide vote for the MVP trophy. Having won the Series MVP award as a member of the Oakland A's in 1973, Jackson became the only player ever to win the award twice. Mr. October delivered again the following autumn, batting .391 with two homers and eight RBIs in New York's six-game World Series victory over the Dodgers. Jackson played most of five tumultuous, drama-filled seasons in New York, his best, statistically, coming in 1980, when he belted 41 homers, batted .300 and drove in 111 runs. He left the Yankees for the California Angels in 1982 and closed his career in 1987 with the A's, the team he started with. Jackson, who ranks sixth on the alltime home run list with 563, and whose .755 Series slugging percentage is the best ever, was inducted into the Hall of Fame in 1993—as a Yankee.

Earning his pinstripes: Jackson entered Yankee lore with his three-homer explosion.

Wilma Unlimited

SEPTEMBER 8, 1960 The most decorated U.S. athlete at the 1960 Olympics was also the one whose childhood predicted the least athletic success. Not only was Wilma Rudolph the 20th of 22 children born to a poor family in rural Tennessee, she was also crippled in childhood by scarlet fever and pneumonia, a combination that rendered her left leg virtually useless.

Despite daily massages from her brothers and sisters, Rudolph wore a leg brace until age 12. Amazingly, she made the 1956 U.S. Olympic team four years after shedding the brace, and when the 1960 Games approached, she had matured into a great champion. She became the first woman to break 23 seconds in the 200, clocking 22.9 at the Olympic trials. But her high hopes seemed dashed when she stepped in a hole near Rome's Olympic Stadium during the Games. "I heard it pop," she said. "I thought I had broken it."

Running the next day on a heavily taped ankle, she tied the 100-meter world record of 11.3. She broke that by three tenths in the final. She won the 200 going away and then anchored the victorious U.S. relay team. Rudolph earned many affectionate nicknames in Rome—the Italian press christened her La Gazzella Nera (the Black Gazelle)—but the best one may have been the one Rudolph chose for herself when she started her own business: Wilma Unlimited.

IN SI'S WORDS

Only America's lovely, graceful girl sprinter, Wilma Rudolph, seemed so clearly the best in her field as [1500 champ Herb] Elliott in his. She was the only athlete in the track and field competition to win three gold medals—in the 100 and 200 meters and in the sprint relay. She is a quiet girl who became even quieter under the stress of sudden fame. Probably the hardest worker on the women's team, she had little time for social life....

After her victories in the two sprints, Wilma anchored the U.S. women's team to a world record (44.4) in the relay. She took the baton even with the second-place German girl. Then, long bronze legs flashing in the straight-up, graceful stride that reminds you of Dave Sime, she moved away easily. Someone asked a French photographer near the finish line, "Who won?" "La Gazelle, naturellement," he said. "La Chattanooga choo-choo."

—Tex Maule, September 12, 1960

Her injured ankle tightly wrapped, Rudolph nonetheless won three gold medals in Rome.

Super Clutch

JULY 9, 1999 Like a kind of sports bra-clad ink blot, Brandi Chastain signified different meanings for different people during her (literal and figurative) moment in the sun after the decisive penalty kick at the 1999 Women's World Cup Final. To some, she was a symbol of powerful femininity. To others she was a role model for millions of girls. Still others saw an endorser, in a brand-name undergarment. To us, she embodied pure clutch.

Think *Time*, *Newsweek* and *People* would have featured a second- or third-place team on their covers? Think again. To take advantage of the Johnny-come-lately media's discovery of women's soccer—where was the press when the U.S. won the first WWC in 1991, or the Olympic gold in '96?—the U.S. *had* to win the tournament. Simply doing well would not be a problem—only two other teams, China and Norway, were in the U.S.'s class—but it would not be enough, either. Only victory would do. One slip-up and all of America would go back to its baseball and its golf, bet on it.

Above all, that's what Chastain symbolized with her now famous jersey-shedding celebration: grace under pressure, mental toughness. When they had to run the table, when not only the world championship but also a brighter future for their sport was on the line, Chastain and her teammates delivered. That's what we call clutch.

SPOTLIGHT

Before her famous penalty kick clinched the 1999 Women's World Cup for the United States, Brandi Chastain scored a tougher and arguably more important goal for her team, in the quarterfinals against Germany.

In the fifth minute, Chastain, a left-sided defender, had misplayed a ball back to U.S. goalkeeper Briana Scurry and accidentally scored on her own team. The gaffe put the U.S. down 1–0. Did Chastain hang her head and allow the mistake to throw her off her game? Not exactly. The U.S. tied the score in the 16th minute but then gave up a morale-wounding goal just before halftime, to go down 2–1. Early in the second half Chastain pounced on a loose ball after a corner kick and ripped a half volley from the top of the box. It bounced off the right post and in. A well-taken and crucial goal. Joy Fawcett scored the winner in the 66th minute, and the U.S. moved on to the semis. Said coach Tony DiCicco of Chastain's tying goal, "I'm really proud of the way Brandi came back."

Chastain became an instant legend.

The Untouchable
Carl Lewis

AUGUST 11, 1984 His manager boasted that after the 1984 Olympics Carl Lewis would be as big as Michael Jackson. And why not? He was handsome and articulate, endowed with a ballet dancer's grace and posture, and a once-in-a-lifetime athletic talent.

No one really came close to touching Lewis in Los Angeles. His first event was the 100, in which he ran 9.99, blowing past Sam Graddy in the final 20 meters to win by eight feet, the largest margin in Olympic history. Up next was the long jump, perhaps Lewis's strongest event. After an opening jump of 28' ¼", which he correctly assumed would be enough to win, Lewis made one more jump then skipped his next four attempts. This was a good common-sense decision, yet fans booed him for not going after Bob Beamon's mythic mark. In the 200 Lewis again won easily, clocking a sensational 19.80 into a headwind.

One supposed there was a slight chance the U.S. team would drop the baton in the relay, costing Lewis a fourth medal. But far from it, the foursome set a world record, and Lewis had his fourth gold, equaling Jesse Owens's storied feat, and he had made it look so easy. Yet for some reason—perhaps those passes in the long jump, perhaps a whiff of excessive smoothness—U.S. fans didn't take to him. They never really did.

IN SI'S WORDS

The imperative of Carl Lewis's chosen race, the 100-meter dash, is simply the imperative of his life. A tall, long-levered man, Lewis must always take a few steps to get those knees up, those arms driving, those hands slicing. He must always reach full speed behind faster starters. And so he must always know that two things will happen over the last 30 meters. His opposition will strain and tighten. And he will not.

This is not a situation for a pinched, panicky soul. This takes obdurate faith in a stillness of mind that allows every muscle except those that throw him forward to stay as loose as lubrication. This takes the absolute dismissal of the grunting sprinters to either side. No issues of manhood are being settled in Lewis's lane. The more purely he runs his race, the more solitary he becomes. The more solitary he becomes, the longer he will last, while othes press and flail and fall behind. Only at the finish, having lasted, is he revealed.

—Kenny Moore, August 20, 1984

Lewis brought the U.S. relay team home in world-record time and won his fourth gold medal.

Did He or Didn't He?

OCTOBER 1, 1932 Whether or not Babe Ruth called his shot in Game 3 of the 1932 World Series against the Cubs, the play was amazing. And, of course, if he did, well, then the feat is audacious, Ruthian, befitting a man whose surname has become an adjective.

The Yankees and Chicago had feuded often, most recently over the Cubs' refusal to grant Mark Koenig, a former Yankee who had joined Chicago for the stretch run, a full share of their postseason bonuses. Before Game 1 Ruth called out to the Cubs dugout, "Hey Mark, who're these cheapskates you're with?"

New York took Games 1 and 2, and when the Series shifted to Wrigley Field for Game 3, and Ruth came to bat in the fifth inning with the score tied 4–4, Chicago fans and players alike were seeing red. Cubs players leaned out of the dugout to berate Ruth, though they could scarcely be heard over the deafening roar of the crowd. Ruth knew what they were doing, though. He took two called strikes and turned to count each one off for the Chicago bench jockeys, while the pitcher, Charlie Root, fumed at the Babe's hot-dogging. Then came the moment of legend: Did Ruth point at the pitcher, or the centerfield bleachers? The truth will never be known, but this much is certain: he belted Root's next offering to deepest centerfield, the longest home run ever at Wrigley Field.

AFTERMATH

Only one newspaper made mention the next day of Ruth's mysterious gesture before his crushing home run, but that was enough to fan the flames of legend. It seems highly unlikely that Ruth called his homer—Hank Aaron believed the mere suggestion to be preposterous—but given the furious jawing between Ruth and the Cubs bench, and the way the Babe rounded the bases after his Bunyan–esque clout—laughing aloud and clasping his hands over his head—it seems safe to say that if the homer wasn't a called shot, it was at least one of the greatest in-your-face moments of all time. Especially when it is recalled that Lou Gehrig hit Root's very next pitch for another home run.

The Yankees won the game 7–5 and swept the Series the next day with a 13–6 rout. It would be Ruth's final appearance in the Fall Classic.

Gehrig (4) congratulated Ruth at home plate.

"Thanks, King."

JULY 15, 1912 The 1912 Olympic Games in Stockholm showcased one of the most remarkable athletes of the century, Jim Thorpe. Part Indian, part Irish and French, Thorpe had lost both his parents while still in his teens and wound up attending the government-run Indian school in Carlisle, Pa. It was there, at the relatively advanced age of 18, that he first discovered his remarkable physical gifts, casually clearing 5'9" in the high jump in his street clothes as the school's high jumpers looked on in awe.

Thorpe first gained national recognition as a football player. In 1911 he scored all 18 points in tiny Carlisle's 18–15 victory over mighty Harvard. He was named All America that year and the next and, believe it or not, he also won the intercollegiate ballroom dancing title in 1912.

In Stockholm, after winning the pentathlon, Thorpe took fourth in the high jump and seventh in the long jump. Then he won the decathlon easily, amassing a world record 8,412 points, 688 ahead of runner-up Hugo Wieslander of Sweden. His score would have placed him second in the *1948* Olympics. Upon presenting Thorpe the gold medal, King Gustav V of Sweden said, "Sir, you are the greatest athlete in the world!" To which the shy Thorpe said, "Thanks, King."

AFTERMATH

Ever the modest country boy, Thorpe was welcomed back home with a ticker tape parade in New York City. "I heard people yelling my name," he later said, "and I couldn't realize how one fellow could have so many friends."

But all that adulation evaporated when, in January 1913, a Massachusetts newspaper revealed that Thorpe had supplemented his income—barely—by playing semi-pro baseball in North Carolina in the summers of 1910 and '11. Thorpe was stripped of his amateur status and his medals.

Still, his athletic career was far from over. He played professional baseball and was a leading figure in the early days of the National Football League. Later he worked as an extra in movies. In 1950 Thorpe was voted the greatest athlete of the first half century in an Associated Press poll. By that time, though, he had sunk to sad depths. When he died in March of 1953 he was a penniless alcoholic living in a California trailer park. The International Olympic Committee restored Thorpe to the record books in 1982 and returned his medals to his family in '83.

Thorpe's decathlon point total was decades ahead of its time.

Stunners

Introduction

Nadia Comaneci stunned Montreal in 1976 with the first perfect scores in Olympics gymnastics history.

Woody Allen once said that in sports you're never ahead of the dramatist. Your favorite basketball team may enter the fourth quarter trailing by 18 points and you may say to yourself, Well, I know how *this* is going to turn out. But unless your favorite team is the Clippers, hold tight. They could come back. You never know. Anything can happen. All the clichés are true.

Of course, the losing team coming back is the exception, not the rule, but that's the point: Fans live for the times they do, the moments when the million-to-one shot comes in a winner. But perhaps a million to one is an exaggeration, because these moments happen with relative regularity. There is a reason you'll never hear sports announcers say a game is in the bag until it is truly in the bag. They've covered enough events to know that they could end up with egg on their face for calling one too early. So, yes, astonishing reversals of fortune, huge upsets, mind-boggling accomplishments occur every season in sports—but still lose none of their power to astonish us.

In the following pages you'll find the times the unexpected took place on the grand stage, with much of the world looking on—sports history's biggest shockers. Like the time Jimmy Valvano and his underdog North Carolina State team knocked off the Phi Slamma Jamma Houston team of Akeem Olajuwon and Clyde Drexler in the NCAA basketball final. Even State's Lorenzo Charles seemed surprised as he grabbed Dereck Whittenburg's errant shot and dropped it into

The U.S. Olympic hockey team (below) shocked the world in 1980, and Steffi Graf (right) stormed her way to a Golden Slam in 1988.

the hoop for the winning points at the buzzer, his eyes wide. Then Valvano took off on his mad dash—sports fans can finish the sentence—looking for someone to hug. Or when Don Larsen, an undistinguished righthander for the Yankees, pitched a perfect game in the 1956 World Series. In the World Series! Never been done before. Hasn't been done since.

Then there is the mother of all Stunners, the moment that SPORTS ILLUSTRATED selected as the greatest athletic accomplishment of the 20th Century: the U.S. Olympic hockey team's upset of the mighty Soviet Union at the 1980 Games in Lake Placid. The U.S. roster was a patchwork of college kids; the Soviets were seasoned pros, Communist economy notwithstanding. One year before the Games, they routed a team of NHL All-Stars, who were in mid-season form, 6–0 at Madison Square Garden. Vyacheslav Fetisov, a

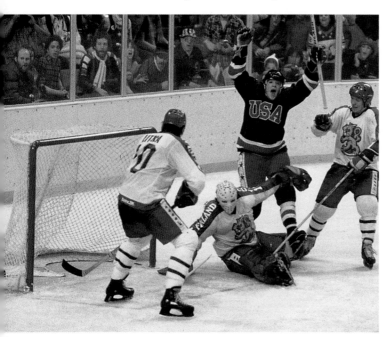

member of the 1980 Soviet team who later won two Stanley Cups with the Detroit Red Wings, said the U.S.S.R. was "the best team ever assembled. And I played for many teams." The Soviets played the U.S. team three days before the Games and whomped them 10–3. So when Mike Eruzione's goal at 10:00 of the third period stood up for a 4–3 victory, make no mistake, an upset of unimaginable proportions had been completed. Forget a million-to-one, this was like a violation of the laws of nature. It simply *shouldn't* have happened. And yet....

Whether they are comebacks, upsets or unprecedented achievements, the moments in our stunners section embody the essence of a fan's love for sports—bearing witness as the utterly improbable comes to pass.

The Miracle Mets

OCTOBER 16, 1969 Former manager Casey Stengel called them "amazin'." That was in 1962, and Stengel meant it ironically. The only thing amazing about those Mets was their ineptitude. They lost 120 games. But now, seven years later, Stengel's irony had twisted further: these Mets *were* amazing. They were a miracle, as others fondly tagged them.

Led by fiery skipper Gil Hodges, the '69 Mets won 38 of their final 50 games to roar back and snatch the NL East from the Chicago Cubs. After sweeping the Braves for the pennant, the Miracle Mets faced the mighty Baltimore Orioles in the World Series.

The Orioles had won 109 games in the regular season and were sure to test the Mets' "miracle" mystique. They did so immediately, with a 4–1 victory in Game 1. But the mystique took hold again and it was all Mets after that. Jerry Koosman hurled a gem to win Game 2, the Series shifted to New York, and the Mets won three straight to wrap it up.

It was a fairy tale with many heroes: outfielders Tommy Agee and Ron Swoboda sparkled defensively, pitcher Tom Seaver went 10 innings in his Game 4 win and Donn Clendenon, the Series MVP, clubbed three home runs. Amazin'.

SPOTLIGHT

No one personified the quiet confidence of the '69 Mets better than 24-year-old pitching star Tom Seaver. In only his third full season in the majors, Seaver established himself as the ace of the Mets staff and one of the most dominant pitchers in the game. With a major league–leading 25 wins and a 2.21 era in '69, Seaver won the first of his three Cy Young Awards.

Mature beyond his years, he was a leader on the mound and in the clubhouse. "When I came to the Mets there was an aura of defeatism on the team; a feeling of let's get it over with," he said. "I could not accept that." He proved as much as the backbone of the Mets staff in '69, and on July 9 against the Cubs, he was nearly flawless: he pitched a perfect game through 8⅓ innings as New York won 4–0. The Mets were rolling and Seaver was their linchpin.

Miracle worker: Seaver was the Mets ace.

Perfection in Montreal

July 19, 1976 "Yes, I was sure," said 14-year-old gymnast Nadia Comaneci. She had just received the fifth of her seven perfect scores and the first of her three gold medals at the 1976 Summer Olympics in Montreal, and someone had asked if she had been confident she would win.

Small wonder, indeed. The 4'11" Romanian had drawn Montreal into her orbit in the 48 hours preceding her victory in the individual all-around competition. She was the undisputed star of the Games, her name on the lips of every fan at the Montreal Forum as she paced on the sidelines before her events.

Comaneci had seized their attention with her performance on the uneven bars, which she approached with trademark stoicism. At points frozen above the bars, at others whirling around one bar, releasing and effortlessly taking hold of the other, she built to a graceful and stunning dismount. Her 23-second routine lacked only what she did not need: hesitation, fear, self-doubt. A heavy pause preceded the score's posting, then up it came—the first perfect 10 in Olympic gymnastic competition. Unfazed, the 86-pound mechanic's daughter from Onesti said, "I knew it was flawless. I have done it 15 times before."

IN SI'S WORDS

Her precision and daring in gymnastics have never been seen before in an Olympics. And few heroines in any sport ever so captivated the Games. She was superbly cast for the moment, bursting upon the world with the first perfect Olympic gymnastic score, a 10.0, on the first day of competition, thereby dramatically ridding Montreal of much of the rancor and turmoil of international politics. Nadia Comaneci was brilliant and beguiling, and because of her youth a great sense of hope and history was instantly attached to her. There was at once the chance to see greatness. For the rare privilege of witnessing the birth of a legend, people splurged $100 on a $16 seat.

—Frank Deford August 2, 1976

Comaneci seemed unafraid of risk and oblivious to pressure.

Jimmy V for Victory

APRIL 4, 1983 What the heck was North Carolina State doing in the NCAA final in the first place? The Wolfpack, coached by Jimmy Valvano, an irrepressible New Yorker, had lost 10 games that year and barely sneaked past three of its foes in the tournament.

Their opponent, the University of Houston, with future NBA Hall of Famers Clyde Drexler and Akeem Olajuwon, was in a different class. Nicknamed Phi Slamma Jamma for their breathtaking aerial game, the Cougars had won 26 straight games and soared easily to the final.

After a lackluster first half, Houston turned a 33–25 deficit into a 42–35 lead. This was what everyone had expected. But Valvano urged his team to work the clock, and send the Cougars to the free-throw line, where they went 10 for 19. State stayed close, and with three seconds to go, it had the ball with the score tied 52–52. Guard Dereck Whittenburg offered up a 35-foot prayer. Houston must have been thinking overtime, because no one boxed out Lorenzo Charles, who plucked the errant shot out of the air and dunked it for the winning bucket. "Akeem didn't see me," Charles said later. "I was up there all by myself."

The last image, amid that sea of delirium, was of Valvano, rushing around all by himself, looking desperately for someone to hug. Who would have guessed he'd need that?

IN SI'S WORDS

You can come out now. The coast is clear. The fraternity party is over. The Houston Phi Slamma Jammas, that Texas chain-saw gang with the tall pledge from Africa in the middle, have finally stopped stuffing college basketball's x's and o's through every hoop they could drape their magnificent bodies over. And curfew came so suddenly: Time running out in the NCAA championship game. A shot in the air. The ball short of the rim. Whooomp!

When the final astounding dunk of the even more astounding 1982-83 season was there for the taking in Albuquerque last Monday night, it was only fitting that an improbable sophomore named Lorenzo Charles, from an even more improbable North Carolina State team was the one to get it. Charles started the season in the doghouse for stealing two pizzas. He ended it in the penthouse by stealing a national title. Or was it in a frat house? ... the new champions had been turned into Theta N.C. State-a.

—Curry Kirkpatrick, April 11, 1983

Charles (43) and Olajuwon (34) appeared equally stunned by the game's final play.

"No Más"

NOVEMBER 25, 1980 Roberto Duran was a warrior and a champion, with a chance to go down as one of the greatest fighters, pound-for-pound, of all time. He had won titles in four weight classes and had whipped Sugar Ray Leonard in their first meeting, in June 1980, handing the Olympic champion his first loss as a pro after 27 victories. But with two small words, Duran threw it all away, and changed the way history will remember him.

In Round 8 of his WBC welterweight title rematch with Leonard in New Orleans, Duran turned his back on his opponent and quit outright. He uttered the words "no más" to referee Octavio Meyran, and Meyran stepped in and signaled one of the strangest endings to a fight in boxing history.

Duran later claimed that stomach cramps forced him out, but many observers believed the real reason was frustration over his inability to hit Leonard. Whereas in their first match Leonard had battled toe-to-toe with Duran—and lost—in the rematch Leonard used his quickness to evade Duran and his boxing skills to score points. The combination KO'd Duran's desire, that night and permanently, it seemed: he never returned to top form, and when he met Leonard for a third time, in 1989, Duran was thoroughly outclassed.

THE OTHER SIDE

When Roberto Duran suddenly quit his WBC welterweight title fight with Sugar Ray Leonard in November 1980, the act somehow sealed Duran's defeat and denied Leonard victory at the same time. Or at least untainted victory. Certainly Leonard won the title, but most boxing fans remember the bout for Duran's quitting rather than for Leonard's winning and avenging the only loss of his career to that point. "I made him quit," Leonard said, but the assertion fell on deaf ears.

Not that the unusual triumph tainted Leonard's legacy. Not in the slightest. After the Duran debacle he quickly established himself as the best in a golden age for the middle weights, an era that included such talents as Thomas Hearns, Marvin Hagler, Wilfred Benitez and Duran. He unified the welterweight title with a 14th-round KO of Hearns in 1981, and went on to win championships in five weight classes during his extraordinary career.

Duran inexplicably turned his back on Leonard in the eighth.

The Playboy's Guarantee

JANUARY 12, 1969 Three days before Super Bowl III, speaking at the Miami Touchdown Club dinner, the Jets' Joe Namath coolly made the kind of put-up-or-shut-up comment that opposing coaches love to post in locker rooms: "We're going to win Sunday. I guarantee it."

No one was quite sure what to make of a guarantee from the playboy quarterback, who caroused and womanized so openly he made it seem almost All-American. The Jets were up against the Baltimore Colts, who'd gone 15–1 that season and were 18-point favorites. One writer predicted a 55–0 rout. Was Namath serious? "We're a better team than Baltimore," he insisted.

Mixing short passes and hand-offs to bruising fullback Matt Snell, Namath drove the Jets 80 yards for an early TD. Jim Turner kicked two field goals and New York led 13–0 in the third quarter. No one knew it, but that would be enough. When the Colts finally scored, with 3:19 left in the game, it was far too late for miracles. The Jets won 16–7.

The playboy had proved he could play with discipline. Namath completed 17 of 28 passes for 206 yards and was voted Super Bowl MVP. This was the game that proved Broadway Joe was much more than just a character.

IN SI'S WORDS

Broadway Joe Namath is the folk hero of the new generation. He is long hair, a Fu Manchu mustache ... swinging night in the live spots of the big city, the dream lover of the stewardi—all that spells insouciant youth in the Jet Age.

Besides all that, Namath is a superb quarterback who in the Super Bowl last week proved that his talent is as big as his mouth—which makes it a very big talent, indeed. He went from Broadway Joe to Super Joe on a cloud-covered afternoon in Miami....

Almost no one thought the New York Jets could penetrate the fine Baltimore defense, but Namath was sure of it and said so.... He was lying by the pool at the Galt Ocean Mile Hotel, where the Jets stayed, tanned and oiled against the sun. Namath reminds you a bit of Dean Martin in his relaxed confidence and in the droop of his heavy-lidded eyes. He is a man of immense self-assurance and, as he showed early in the week, a man of startling honesty.

—Tex Maule, January 20, 1969

Namath talked it, then walked it.

A Golden Oldie

APRIL 13, 1986 Jack Nicklaus as the underdog? Come on, the Golden Bear? Winner of 17 major professional titles? Fat chance. For a quarter century, Nicklaus had dominated the game of golf like no other, routinely and ruthlessly dispatching one rival after another. But when the 1986 Masters began, Nicklaus was six years removed from his last major victory; the Golden Bear had lost some of his luster. "Jack's got to start thinking about when it is time to retire," said CBS golf analyst Ken Venturi.

Suddenly, it became a whole lot easier to root for Nicklaus. He was 46, and on his way out, right? Wrong. Nicklaus shot a 69 on Saturday and began the final round only four strokes off the pace. He made a birdie at No. 9, rolled in a 25-foot putt for birdie at 10, and followed that with another birdie at 11. By the time Nicklaus reached the 16th tee after an eagle at 15, the gallery was roaring its approval. He came within inches of a hole-in-one. On 17, he drained an 11-foot putt to take the lead and he capped his record-tying back nine (30) with a solid par at 18. Augusta National was bedlam. Twenty-three years after his first Masters title, Nicklaus had won a record sixth green jacket. "I finally found that guy I used to know on the golf course," Nicklaus said. "It was me."

THE OTHER SIDE

"One of these days I'm going to break his record of six Masters," Greg Norman promised after the 1986 Masters. Norman, the handsome blond Australian nicknamed the Shark, was emerging as the finest golfer of his generation, and needed only a par on 18 to force a playoff with Jack Nicklaus at Augusta in '86. But Norman sliced his second shot into the gallery and had to settle for a bogey and second place. Still, few doubted that Norman would be back. He was only 31.

But Augusta National would not be kind to Norman in the future either. In 1987, the Shark lost a sudden-death playoff when Larry Mize drained a 140-foot chip shot. In 1996, he turned a six-stroke lead into a five-stroke deficit with a final round 78. Norman would never get those six Masters, and his legacy of tragic near-misses would become legend. Seven times Norman would enter the Sunday of a major with a lead, and only once (at the 1986 British Open) would he win.

At 46, Nicklaus became the oldest golfer ever to win the Masters.

Crowning Glory

JUNE 9, 1973 By 10 a.m. on the day of the 105th running of the Belmont Stakes, an oppressive humidity had descended upon Elmont, New York, site of the race. And Secretariat, the favorite to win and thereby capture the first Triple Crown victory in 25 years, was as hot as the weather. "If he wants to run early, let him," trainer Lucien Laurin told jockey Ron Turcotte.

Sure enough, Secretariat bolted from the gate at full throttle, bringing the crowd of nearly 70,000 to its feet. But the red-hot colt was not alone. After 220 yards, Sham, with Laffit Pincay Jr. up, flew into the lead by a head. The pair ran the opening quarter mile in:

23⅗. The already relentless pace had quickened by the one-mile mark, causing one spectator to gasp, "They're going too fast!"

But Secretariat sailed effortlessly along under Turcotte, who let the horse have his race. When Sham's legs turned to rubber heading into the backstretch, the track belonged to Secretariat. With the clock as his only competitor, the incomparable colt stretched his lead to 28, 29, 30 and finally 31 lengths. Racing veterans blinked incredulously not only at the timer—which registered a track record 2:24—but also at the new standard Secretariat had set for horse-racing greatness.

Turcotte (above) and Secretariat won the Belmont by the widest margin in Triple Crown history.

"His only point of reference is himself."

—Charles Hatton,
former *Daily Racing Form*
columnist, on Secretariat

AFTERMATH

Secretariat's owner Penny Tweedy had offered shares of her big red colt in early 1973, and after the Belmont Stakes, they exploded in value to $500,000 apiece. The horse was on pace to earn more than $850,000 by the end of the season.

After winning a second consecutive Horse of the Year award, Secretariat left racing in November '73. The colt capped his career with a win at the Canadian International Championship, then retired to the Claiborne stud farm in Paris, Kentucky, where he sired more than 650 offspring, including 57 stakes winners, while fetching stud fees of $75,000.

Secretariat was put down on October 2, 1989, after a bout with laminitis, a hoof disease. His Kentucky Derby and Belmont Stakes track records have stood for more than 26 years.

Secretariat set a fast pace out of the gate, and maintained it throughout the race.

"Do You Believe In Miracles?"

FEBRUARY 22, 1980 No one on the ice had any illusions about who was who: The Americans knew they were underdogs; the Soviets knew they were heavy favorites. The Soviets were grizzled pros, products of a rigid state system. They had routed the NHL All-Stars, and they had trounced this very U.S. team 10–3 prior to the Games.

But the U.S. players weren't all that helpless. Their coach, Herb Brooks, used a 300-question psychological test to help pick his players. He had also whipped them into superb shape with endless sprints they came to call Herbies. Before the game Brooks told his team, "This is your moment and it's going to happen."

The biggest goal of the game may have been the one by Mark Johnson that tied the score 2–2 at the first-period buzzer. Johnson again tied the game, 3–3, in the third, to set the stage for Mike Eruzione's wrist shot past Soviet goalie Vladimir Myshkin with 10 minutes left. U.S. 4, Soviet Union 3. Those 10 minutes seemed to last forever. Finally, it ended, and spontaneous celebrations ignited all around the U.S. In their locker room after the game, the U.S. team broke into *God Bless America*. It was one of those surreal moments, treasured by sports fans, when everybody went a little crazy.

IN SI'S WORDS

For millions of people, their single, lasting image of the Lake Placid Games will be the infectious joy displayed by the U.S. hockey team following its 4–3 win over the Soviet Union last Friday night. It was an Olympian moment, the kind the creators of the Games must have had in mind, one that said: Here is something that is bigger than any of you. It was bizarre, it was beautiful. Upflung sticks slowly cartwheeled into the rafters. The American players —in pairs rather than in one great glop—hugged and danced and rolled on one another.

The Soviet players, slightly in awe, it seemed, of the spectacle of their defeat, stood in a huddle near their blue line, arms propped on their sticks, and waited for the ceremonial postgame handshakes with no apparent impatience. There was no head-hanging. This was bigger, even, than the Russians. "The first Russian I shook hands with had a smile on his face," said Mark Johnson, who had scored two of the U.S. goals. "I couldn't believe it. I still can't believe it. We beat the Russians."

—E.M. Swift, March 3, 1980

The game-winner beat Myshkin with 10 minutes left.

Tough Luck
Billy Buck

OCTOBER 25, 1986 A career .289 hitter who led the league in batting in 1980 and hit .323 in '78, Bill Buckner unfortunately will always be best remembered for one moment of infamy during Game 6 of the 1986 World Series against the New York Mets.

On a crisp evening in New York, the Red Sox led 5–3 in the bottom of the 10th and were one out away from winning their first World Series since 1918. Successive singles by Gary Carter and Kevin Mitchell kept the Mets' faint hopes alive. Ray Knight blooped another single and suddenly, New York was down by one with men on first and third. Bob Stanley came in to face Mookie Wilson and threw a wild pitch to bring in the tying run. The stage was set for Buckner's gaffe.

Wilson trickled a grounder toward first. Buckner crouched to make the play, but the ball squirted under his glove, between his legs and into rightfield. Knight raced home with the winning run. "I can't remember the last time I missed a ground ball," Buckner said. But fans—particularly Boston fans—and the media would never let him forget this one. There were plenty of culprits in Boston's collapse, but Buckner's glaring error made him the perfect fit for the goat horns.

Certainly not the parting shot his distinguished 22-year career deserved.

AFTERMATH

Following their improbable comeback victory in Game 6, the New York Mets played come-from-behind baseball again in the deciding Game 7.

The Red Sox jumped out to a three-run lead on home runs by Rich Gedman and Dwight Evans, and starting pitcher Bruce Hurst held the Mets scoreless through five. That's when things began to unravel for Boston. The Mets knocked Hurst out of the game with three runs in the sixth inning to tie the score. They again victimized the Boston bullpen in the seventh, scoring three more runs to go ahead 6–3. Boston rallied for two runs in the top of the eighth to pull within one, but the Mets piled on two runs in their half and held on for the 8–5 victory.

After making the final pitch, New York closer Jesse Orosco flung his glove skyward in celebration. The Mets had captured their first World Series since 1969, and like that memorable edition of the team, had benefited from a few miracles along the way.

Curse of the Bambino? Buckner's error extended Boston's World Series futility.

A Golden Slam

OCTOBER 1, 1988 "I played Steffi when she was 12 and so tiny I could hardly see her over the net," Eva Pfaff of Germany once said. "She was running into the corners all the time. I couldn't imagine she had such a forehand, but I found out. I won very close. Three years later we played again. It was like I was nonexistent on the court."

Steffi Graf won her first title when she was 16, and by the time she was 20 she had won 36. Her competition was as Pfaff had felt: nonexistent. In 1988, at 19, she captured a prize so rare it had eluded Billie Jean King, Chris Evert and Martina Navratilova: tennis's Grand Slam. She even went one better; after taking all four majors, Graf won the Olympic singles title.

She began her quest by downing Evert 6–1, 7–6 for the Australian Open title. At the French Open, she overwhelmed Natalia Zvereva 6–0, 6–0 for the first shutout in a major final since 1911. It took 32 minutes. Navratilova pushed her at Wimbledon, taking the first set, 7–5, but Graf swept the next two 6–2, 6–1. In the U.S. Open final, Graf met Gabriela Sabatini, who had defeated her twice that year. With the first Grand Slam in 18 years in sight, Graf did not falter, winning 6–3, 3–6, 6–1. Then it was off to Seoul for the cherry on top: a gold medal after another victory over Sabatini, 6–3, 6–3.

Fräulein Forehand owned tennis in 1988.

Perfect

OCTOBER 8, 1956 The first two batters were named Junior and Pee Wee, and they both struck out, setting the tone for a day in which all of the Dodgers batters would be as boys before the man on the mound, Don Larsen of the New York Yankees.

A 6' 4" righthander, Larsen had had an unremarkable career since his debut for St. Louis in 1953. He'd had an unremarkable World Series, too, having been routed out of Game 2 in the second inning as the Yankees lost 13–8. But when New York rallied to win Games 3 and 4 and tie the Series at two games apiece, Yankees manager Casey Stengel stuck with Larsen for the fifth game.

He set down the boyishly monikered Gilliam and Reese and never looked back, retiring 27 straight batters to secure both the first no-hitter and the first perfect game in World Series history. With the Yanks ahead 2–0 in the ninth, he retired Carl Furillo and Roy Campanella to bring up pinch hitter Dale Mitchell. He threw his first pitch for a ball, his second for a called strike. A swinging strike two, then a foul ball, then Larsen, pitching from the stretch as he had all day, reared back and zinged a fastball for a called strike three. As the crowd erupted, Yogi Berra raced out from behind the plate and leaped into his pitcher's arms.

AFTERMATH

Despite the blow that Don Larsen's perfect game must have been to their psyches, the gritty Dodgers battled back and won Game 6 to even the Series at three games each. This one, too, was a pitching classic, as the Yanks Bob Turley and Brooklyn's Clem Labine both pitched shutout ball through nine innings. In the tenth, Jackie Robinson smacked a liner to left to bring Junior Gilliam in from second for the game's only run. But Brooklyn would crash in Game 7, a 9–0 rout for the Yankees in which Yogi Berra smacked two two-run homers and Moose Skowron belted a grand slam. The Yankees had avenged their Series loss to Brooklyn the previous year.

Larsen never won more than 10 games in a season after 1956, and was traded to Kansas City in 1960. He retired in 1967 at age 38. Amazingly, the next Yankee to pitch a perfect game, David Wells, who spun his perfecto in 1998, went to the same high school as Larsen, Point Loma in San Diego.

The scoreboard tells the tale of Larsen's perfection.

The Fall of Iron Mike

FEBRUARY 10, 1990 Mike Tyson had scored 33 knockouts while running his record to 37–0. But Tyson had more than just a great record. He had an aura: He was brutality incarnate, squat and muscled and ready to take heads off. He had dispatched Michael Spinks in just 91 seconds. By the time he faced the unheralded Buster Douglas in Tokyo, Tyson was widely regarded as invincible.

Douglas, for his part, was practically invisible. When he arrived at the weigh-in, not one photographer bothered to take a picture. His main qualifications for this bout seemed to be his availability and pay scale. The strategy he announced did little to persuade anyone he had a chance. "I'll just hit him, I guess," shrugged the 29-year-old 233-pounder from Columbus, Ohio.

From the start, Douglas hit Tyson with rights, using his height advantage. But Tyson dropped Douglas at the end of Round 8, and Douglas may have been saved by the referee's delayed count. He got to his feet at nine. The escape seemed to energize him, because in the next round he battered the champ's left eye shut, and in the 10th he stunned Tyson with a vicious uppercut. Then he floored him with a chopping left hook. Tyson, who had never before touched the canvas, was beyond helping himself. He got to his feet and stumbled into the ref's embrace, invincible no more.

IN SI'S WORDS

Tyson, who had never before been knocked down in his professional career, skidded on his backside. As referee Octavio Meyran Sánchez began the 10 count, Tyson flipped himself over and began sweeping the canvas with his right arm. A boxer's reflex is a strange and revealing thing. Finally, Tyson found his mouthpiece, started to insert it backward into his mouth and then desperately climbed to his feet and into Meyran's protective embrace, his good eye fogged in a way you cannot imagine.

This is how the latest of sports' sure things, the Tyson dynasty, ended: far from home and entirely removed from expectation and possibility, well short of a $70 million ... bout this spring with Evander Holyfield and a subsequent program of purportedly easier assignments in other countries. It was probably the biggest upset in boxing history, and certainly the unlikeliest result of all recent sporting events."

—Richard Hoffer, February 19, 1990

It was all downhill for Tyson after his shocking loss to Douglas.

Mark's Magnificent 7

SEPTEMBER 4, 1972 "I swam my brains out," said Mark Spitz of his seven-gold-medal triumph at the Munich Olympics. Spitz won the 100- and 200-meter freestyles, the 100- and 200-meter butterflys and swam a leg on three winning relay teams. Having also—unbelievably—broken seven world records, Spitz became the dashing American hero of an otherwise tragically marred Olympics: 11 Israeli athletes were kidnapped and murdered by Palestinian terrorists during the Games.

Spitz had not always been the favorite. During the 1968 Olympics in Mexico City, as a brash 18-year-old, he boasted that he would win six gold medals. After a "disappointing" haul of two relay golds, an individual silver and bronze, Spitz threw himself into four more years of intensive training under the renowned University of Indiana coach Doc Counsilman.

Following his father's maxim, "Swimming isn't everything; winning is," Spitz trained his way to his '72 Olympic triumph. His success was further crowned by corporate sponsors, and Spitz blazed a trail as a millionaire athlete endorser. Almost 30 years later, the image of a tanned Spitz, grinning broadly, wearing only his stars-and-stripes swimsuit and seven gold medals around his neck, remains indelibly etched in the American memory.

SPOTLIGHT

The Cold War was at its bristled height when mustachioed Mark Spitz—a 22-year-old Olympic hopeful and California native—asked the Russian swim team, which was practicing at the time, if he could have 15 minutes of pool time. This was a few days before Spitz won the first of his seven gold medals at the Munich Games. Ceding him an outside lane, the Russians promptly began photographing his powerful stroke. Spitz obliged with a bizarre performance, and blithely answered the Russian coach's queries afterwards. "I started telling him it was a new technique to gain muscle by swimming inefficiently. I was just making this up. Then he said, 'And doesn't your mustache drag water?' I said, 'No it actually deflects water from my mouth and allows me to keep my head in a lower position that helps my speed.' [The coach] repeats everything in Russian to some guy taking notes. The next year, Vladimir Bure, a top Russian swimmer, shows up to competition with a mustache."

Spitz brightened up an otherwise gloomy Games.

Teddy Ballgame

SEPTEMBER 28, 1941 He was hitting .438 in June, and some people wondered if he might break Hugh Duffy's record of .440, set in 1894. That was wishful thinking, of course, but Ted Williams went swinging through August at .414 and into September with a chance to become the first man in 11 years to bat .400 for a season. Eleven years may not seem like a long time, but when you consider that no one has batted .400 since 1941—a span of 59 years and counting—you get an idea of how difficult it is to achieve.

Heading into Boston's season-ending series with the Philadelphia A's, Williams's average stood at .401. He went 1 for 4 in the first game and it dipped to .39955. His manager, Joe Cronin, offered to bench him for the last two games, a Sunday doubleheader. If Williams sat, his season average would be rounded up to .400.

He didn't even consider it. Grabbing the pressure by the throat, he belted a single in his first at-bat, then homered and hit two more singles. The 4-for-5 day boosted his average to .404. Sit out the nightcap? Nah. Williams again singled in his first at-bat, and the Sox swept. The Kid had gone 6 for 8 with four singles, a double and a home run. His average was .406. "I gave it a good day," he said. "Not a bad day at all."

IN SI'S WORDS

Williams was scheduled to face one of Mr. [Connie] Mack's rookies, Dick Fowler, and Ted says that facing a rookie is always at least one lost at-bat until you figure him out. Williams was greeted at the plate by A's catcher Frankie Hayes, who told him, "Mr. Mack says we have to go right after you and pitch to you." That was good news: In earlier games this season Mr. Mack's particular idea of putting the shift on Williams was to relocate the strike zone to Delaware County. In their last eight games with Boston, the A's pitchers had walked Williams 14 times.

So his first time up against Fowler, Williams greeted a strike like a gift and rifled a drive in the hole between first and second for a single. That may or may not have lifted him over .400. Before we [in the press box] could calculate it, the Kid homered and then singled two more times.

—Richard Hoffer, July 19, 1993.
[The author "returned to yesteryear" to report on Williams's memorable achievement.]

Nobody loved to hit more than Williams.

Playing Against Type

FEBRUARY 25, 1964 The picture has been repainted drastically by history's hand, but here's how it looked in 1964: Sonny Liston, the fearsome heavyweight champion with the 17½-inch neck and the 15-inch fists, was going to knock out the 22-year-old pretty boy Cassius Clay. It wasn't a matter of if Liston would deck Clay, it was a matter of when. He was a 7-to-1 favorite.

Clay, who would later change his name to Muhammad Ali, was a brash, trash-talking Olympic gold medalist with a flashy, unorthodox style. He sometimes fought with his hands at his sides and relied on his quickness to both deliver and avoid punches from that posture. Boxing experts frankly didn't take him seriously.

Liston, on the other hand, was a heavy puncher coming off two consecutive first-round knockouts of the respected former champ, Floyd Patterson. This one wasn't going to be close.

And it wasn't: The faster, younger Clay pounded Liston for six rounds. When the champ, bloodied over both eyes and suffering from a torn left biceps, failed to answer the bell for Round 7, what many considered the greatest upset in the sport's history was complete. Of course, Ali soon made us all forget that he ever could have been cast as an underdog.

IN SI'S WORDS

Cassius Clay, who for weeks had cried, "Float like a butterfly, sting like a bee," floated and stung—and he whipped Sonny Liston as thoroughly as a man can be whipped....

For weeks, comment on the outcome of the fight had centered on the number of minutes Clay could avoid Liston's fearsome left hand. For the whole first round, those watching ... were on the edges of their seats, expecting at any moment that Clay, a feather-footed, fluidly graceful man dancing around the perimeter of disaster, would slip or falter and that one of the vicious, brutal punches that Liston launched in an endless series would catch him....

[After the bout] Liston sat limp and slumped down, tears trickling over his battered cheeks. It seemed incredible, looking at him, that this was the same frightening specter who had entered the ring 20 minutes earlier. It seemed wrong, somehow, to feel sorry for Sonny Liston.

—Tex Maule, March 9, 1964

Clay was too quick and too skilled for Liston.

Recordbreakers

Introduction

Records are the most fascinating of athletic achievements. They are quite simply the yard-sticks we use to measure the outer limits of human performance.

But records tell us little about future potential. For years, scientists and coaches declared

it physically impossible for a man to run a mile in under four minutes. "Whether as athletes we liked it or not, the four-minute mile had become rather like an Everest—a challenge to the human spirit," wrote Roger Bannister in his autobiography, *The Four Minute Mile.* "It was a barrier that seemed to defy all attempts to break it—an irksome reminder that man's striving might be in vain." But empiricists—runners like Bannister—knew this was nonsense, and on May 6, 1954, he proved it so by running 3:59.4.

One of the more intriguing questions about record-setting is the interplay of expectation and performance. To put it another way: Does our knowledge of records limit us in our pursuit of them? Why can't some swimmer possessed of a genius imagination project herself into the future and, by thinking like a swimmer from 2050, swim like one today? Somehow, the mind balks at the suggestion.

Was that Bob Beamon's secret? In 1968, in the thin air of Mexico City Beamon improved the world long jump record by an incomprehensible 21¾", casting any notion of orderly progression to the winds. His jump was a blow not for evolution, but revolution. Was it a leap of imagination as well as feet and inches?

Despite Beamon's example, we still assume that records will fall in some reassuringly predictable fashion. If one man or woman can

Cal Ripken's record of 2,632 consecutive games played is sure to stand for decades.

do something, why can't another do it slightly better? Still, certain records do seem unbreakable, not because athletes aren't improving, but because the games have changed. Wilt Chamberlain's 100-point game in 1962 seems more untouchable than ever; in fact no *two* teammates have combined for 100 points in a game since. And with scoring dwindling to the point where the average NBA game sees both teams hover near 100, Wilt's record seems safe. So do Byron Nelson's record of 11 straight PGA tournament victories in 1945, and Joe DiMaggio's 1941 streak of hitting safely in 56 consecutive baseball games.

Equally fascinating is the investment we all seem to have in certain records. The entire country cheered for Mark McGwire's every homer, it seemed, as he chased Roger Maris's single-season home run record in 1998. The grotesque underbelly of our strange personal investment in records displayed itself in the racist hate mail Hank Aaron received as he neared Babe Ruth's career mark of 714 homers.

Unlike our other recordbreakers, the Miami Dolphins of 1972-73 marched to his-

tory as a team. They had company as they chased the only undefeated season in NFL history. As all of our recordbreakers can attest, it gets awfully lonely out there, charting the outer limits of human performance.

Martina Navratilova won a record nine Wimbledons.

Tigermania

APRIL 13, 1997 When Jack Nicklaus played a practice round at Augusta with Tiger Woods and Arnold Palmer in 1996 and speculated that the 20-year-old star could one day win more Masters then he and Palmer had won combined, people scoffed. That would give Woods 10 green jackets. But no one was laughing as Woods's final, four-foot putt rolled into the cup on that Sunday afternoon in 1997.

During four days of splendid golf, Woods destroyed the Masters field by 12 strokes and bested the tournament record of 271, held by Raymond Floyd and Nicklaus, with an 18-under 270. His titantic drives off the tee made childs' play of Augusta's mammoth par-5's. By Sunday afternoon, he had practically made the course obsolete. "Unless they build Tiger tees about 50 yards back, he's going to win the next 20 of these," said Jesper Parnevik, who finished 19 strokes behind Woods.

Revolutions don't happen every day—especially in the genteel sport of golf. But Tiger Woods's performance at the 1997 Masters sent shock waves

Woods's records during his dominating 1997 Masters: youngest winner (21), lowest score (270) and widest margin of victory (12 strokes).

"He said the best shot he saw all week was the shot of me hugging my dad."

— Tiger Woods,
describing President Clinton's reaction
to Woods's 1997 Masters victory.

IN SI'S WORDS

So golf is trying to get used to the fact that the man who will rule the game for the next 20 years shaves twice a week and has been drinking legally for almost three months now.... It was something to see the way a 6'2", 155-pounder with a 30-inch waist crumbled one of golf's masterpieces into bite-sized pieces. The longest club he hit into a par-4 all week was a seven-iron. On each of the first two days he hit a wedge into the 500-yard par-5 15th hole—for his second shot. Honey, he shrunk the course. Last Saturday his seven birdies were set up by his nine-iron, pitching wedge, sand wedge, putter, nine-iron, putter and sand wedge. Meanwhile, the rest of the field was trying to catch him with five-irons and three-woods and rosary beads.

—Rick Reilly, April 21, 1997

through the game. He was young (21), he was multiracial, and he had just shredded the sport's most hallowed course, along with some of its outdated mores (Augusta didn't sign its first minority member until 1991). Augusta National, and the sport of golf, were changed forever.

Woods was the center of attention at Augusta (right), and he handled the pressure with a smile.

The Four-Minute Mile

MAY 6, 1954 Roger Bannister worried about the wind on that memorable May morning. He spent the day monitoring the trees, the flags, the scarves on people he passed on the street. Would the wind permit him to do what was considered impossible only 10 years earlier: run a mile in under four minutes?

It was not until Bannister took his place on the starting line of Oxford's Iffley Road track—and saw that the flag atop a nearby church was still—that he decided the attempt was on. When he came past the timers at the quarter-mile mark, Bannister heard 57.5. Perfect. He reached the half mile in 1:58, perfect again, and passed three quarters at 3:00.7. He knew he needed to run a 59-second final lap.

"Those last few seconds seemed never-ending," Bannister later wrote. "The faint line of … tape stood ahead as a haven of peace, after the struggle." He crossed the line and collapsed, knowing only that he must have come close.

The charm of that day's momentous event was heightened by the meet announcer, who informed the crowd that it was, a "new stadium, meet, English, European, Commonwealth and, subject to ratification, world record. The time was three—." His next words were lost in delirious cheers. We know the time very well, though. It was 3:59.4, and it will never be forgotten.

AFTERMATH

Who knows how much longer Bannister might have run had he not settled, once and for all, the question of whether a man can run a mile in under four minutes. He retired after the 1954 season, but not before running one of the greatest, most competitive races of the century in August at the Empire Games in Vancouver, Canada. Bannister's main opponent was John Landy, the Australian whom he had feared might beat him to the great barrier. And with good reason: only 46 days after Bannister's great race at Oxford, Landy ran 3:58.0.

The bookmakers annointed Landy a 4–1 favorite, and he took the race out hard, leading Bannister by 15 yards in the second lap. Slowly Bannister ran him down until, coming off the final bend, he was sitting on Landy's shoulder. Here Landy made a classic tactical error, glancing back over his inside shoulder. Seeing this, Bannister surged around him, and won in 3:58.8, five yards ahead of Landy. Both men had broken four.

Bannister broke the tape, and a landmark barrier.

Oh, Henry!

APRIL 8, 1974 Henry Aaron began the 1973 season 41 homers short of Babe Ruth's career record of 714, and immediately went on a tear, belting 11 home runs by mid-May. But as the 39-year-old Aaron heated up, so too did the hate mail he received, full of threats and racial slurs, from bigots who couldn't bear to see a black man break Ruth's hallowed record.

There were millions of fans who wished him well, but the thousands of hate letters hurt Aaron deeply, transforming what should have been the most enjoyable time in his career into a pressure-packed nightmare. Amazingly, he belted 40 homers in '73, and entered the following season needing one to tie, two to break the most famous record in baseball.

Aaron wasted no time, tying Ruth with his very first swing of the new season, against the Reds. He passed the Bambino in the fourth inning of the Braves' home opener against the Dodgers, on a 1–0 fastball from Al Downing. Aaron lashed the ball in a looping arc over the leftfield fence and into the Braves' bullpen, where it was retrieved by reliever Tom House. House clutched the artifact and sprinted to home plate to present it to the new home run king, who was being mobbed by fans and teammates. "I just thank God it's all over," said Aaron. An undeservedly bittersweet ending to a magnificent journey.

THE OTHER SIDE

Guy Bush, Tracy Stallard, and Al Downing (and now, Steve Trachsel). Besides successful major league pitching careers, these men also have in common the distinction of being answers to well-known baseball trivia questions. Bush gave up Babe Ruth's 714th home run; Stallard served up Roger Maris's 61st clout in 1961 (Trachsel threw Mark McGwire's 62nd in 1998); and Downing delivered what would be Hank Aaron's 715th home run, arguably the most famous pitch in baseball history.

Saying he would pitch Aaron "no differently tonight," Downing walked Hammerin' Hank his first time up, then gave up the historic clout in the fourth. "It was a fastball down the middle…." Downing said. "I was trying to get it down … but I didn't."

Before the game Downing had said "I think people will remember the pitcher who throws the last one he ever hits, not the 715th."

He was wrong about that.

Aaron felt relief rather than joy after breaking Ruth's home run record.

Sharecroppers' Son

AUGUST 4, 1936 Never has an Olympic athlete been thrust onto a stage quite like the one that awaited Jesse Owens at the Berlin Games of 1936. He was expected not only to win four gold medals—in the 100, 200, long jump and relay—but also to disprove the odious racial theories of the century's greatest villain.

The son of sharecroppers and grandson of slaves, Owens had won the 100, 200 and long jump at the U.S. Olympic trials, a feat that surprised no one who knew what he'd done a year earlier, while competing for Ohio State at the Big Ten championships. In a 45-minute span, Owens broke or tied six world records.

In Berlin, he won the two dashes and the sprint relay as easily as expected, breaking two Olympic and one world record along the way. The long jump was trickier. After apparently being duped out of one attempt by the German officials and fouling on another, Owens was approached by the German jumper Luz Long, who chatted with him and then suggested he move his steps back to avoid fouling. Owens qualified easily and went on to beat Long in the final.

Owens won four gold medals at the 1936 Games, breaking one world and two Olympic records.

"Jesse Owens is still the same to me, a legend. I'm just a person with some God-given talent."

— Carl Lewis,
after his four-gold-medal
performance in 1984

Legend has it that Hitler snubbed Owens by refusing to meet him after honoring three other winners. Owens preferred to dwell on the kindness of a man who had much to lose. "You can melt down all the medals and cups I have," he wrote, "and they wouldn't be a plating on the 24-carat friendship I felt for Luz Long at that moment."

AFTERMATH

Luz Long's gesture of sportsmanship to Jesse Owens, in the face of tremendous racist propaganda, is surely one of the most moving expressions of the Olympic ideal. A grateful Owens remained friendly with Long right up to the day the German was killed in World War II. After that he continued to correspond with Long's family.

After the Games Owens was ignored by both Franklin Delano Roosevelt and the AAU, which gave the 1936 Sullivan Award to decathlon champ Glenn Morris. Struggling financially, Owens later raced for money against dogs, horses and motorcycles. He eventually achieved financial stability by giving motivational speeches to business groups.

In 1968 Owens angered some black Americans by siding with the Olympic Committee following the Black Power demonstration at the Mexico City Olympics. Before dying from lung cancer in 1980, Owens renounced that position too, in his book *I Have Changed*.

In a Berlin saturated with Nazi propaganda, the German people nevertheless embraced Owens (above middle, and right, winning a heat in the 200) as the hero of the Games.

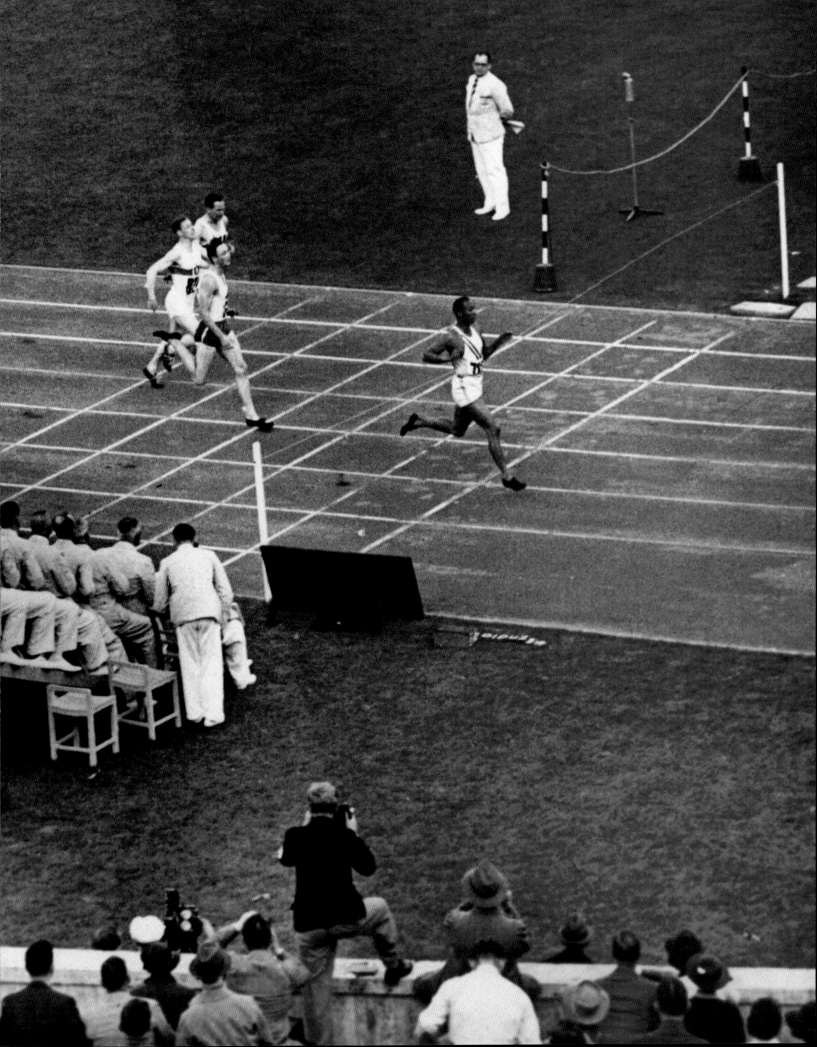

Ninety-Two
for No. 99

MARCH 28, 1982 Wayne Gretzky's career has great moments like Bill Gates has dollars. Selecting one as the greatest is like staring into a sack of diamonds—you could go blind from the glare.

When he joined the NHL from the defunct WHA, where he had scored 110 points the previous year, skeptics said, No way that skinny 18-year-old does that in *this* league. Gretzky scored *137* points on 51 goals and 86 assists in his first NHL season.

Of course he was just getting started. He would go on to rewrite the NHL record book, win nine MVP awards during the 1980s, and lead his team to four Stanley Cup titles. Gretzky picked the first of those team triumphs as his greatest moment, but the jewel we've selected is his 1981-82 season.

That was the year he scored 50 goals in his first 39 games to obliterate the previous mark of 50 in 50 held by Rocket Richard and Mike Bossy. That was the year he broke Phil Esposito's single-season goals record of 76, in just 64 games. That was the year he finished with a previously unimaginable 92 goals—the 92nd coming in a 6–2 romp by Edmonton over Los Angeles—in 80 games. He also had 120 assists for a record 212 points.

Yes, Gretzky is filthy rich with shining moments, but none sparkles brighter than 92 in '82.

THE OTHER SIDE

What was it like to face Wayne Gretzky? According to New Jersey Devils defenseman Scott Stevens, it could be scary: "He used to sort of pop up unexpectedly, like a monster in a tunnel of horrors at an amusement park. When you saw who it was, it sort of scared the devil out of you."

"It's no good trying to line him up for a hard check; he's too mobile," said Boston center Dave Kasper. "If you start lunging at him, he'll make you look ridiculous."

Former Canadiens goalie Ken Dryden said, "He has an enormous sense of patience.... When he comes down the ice, there's a point when the defenseman thinks: He's going to commit himself one way or the other now. When that moment passes and Gretzky still hasn't committed, the whole rhythm of the game is upset. The defenseman is unprepared for what might come next. It's not an anticlimax. It's *beyond* the climax. And suddenly a player becomes open who wasn't open before."

Gretzky's 77th goal in 1981–82—which broke Phil Esposito's single-season record of 76—came against Buffalo in the Great One's 64th game of the season.

Fifty-Six in a Row for Joltin' Joe

JULY 16, 1941 The nation was on the brink of war, but the question on everyone's lips in the summer of 1941 was, "Did DiMaggio get a hit today?" To say that Joe DiMaggio was on a hot streak would have been like saying that his future wife, Marilyn Monroe, was kind of attractive. The Yankee Clipper was on fire.

On July 2, the 26-year-old hit safely in his 45th straight game, belting a home run against Boston to break Wee Willie Keeler's 44-year-old major-league record. He didn't stop there. Despite losing his favorite bat to a souvenir hunter the day he broke Keeler's record, DiMaggio kept banging out hits. He swung his way past 50 games and kept going. In his 54th, the streak nearly ended when he topped a roller toward third and barely beat it out for his only hit of the day. Entering the Yankees' game on July 17 against the Indians, Joltin' Joe had produced a hit in 56 straight games.

Alas, in front 67,468 fans at Cleveland's Municipal Stadium, the mighty streak came to an end. DiMaggio twice sent rockets down the third base line that looked like sure hits, only to be robbed by Cleveland third baseman Ken Keltner. With the bases loaded in the eighth, DiMaggio grounded out. The Yanks won the game 4–3, but Joe D's wish that the Streak "could have gone on forever" would not come true.

AFTERMATH

In addition to depriving him of a chance to push the streak past 60 games, DiMaggio's July 17th o-fer against Cleveland may have cost him financially. If he had extended the streak to 57 games, the Heinz company, makers of Heinz 57 sauce, was rumored to have a $10,000 endorsement offer ready.

Incredibly, the day after being held hitless by the Indians, Joltin' Joe, with his trusty bat back in his possession (the fan who had filched it on July 2 returned it), embarked on another streak, this one lasting 16 games. When the second run ended, DiMaggio had hit safely in an astounding 72 of 73 games.

During the 56-game streak, DiMaggio batted .408 with 15 home runs. His record may not be untouchable, but it will be extremely difficult to match, to say the least. From 1941 to 2000, only Pete Rose of the Cincinnati Reds had even approached DiMaggio's mark. In 1978, Rose hit safely in 44 consecutive games to tie Willie Keeler for the National League record.

No one had a sweeter stroke than the Yankee Clipper.

The Queen of Center Court

JULY 7, 1990 Zina Garrison had knocked off two of the top players in the world, Steffi Graf and Monica Seles, to reach the final, but Martina Navratilova didn't care. No matter how well the 26-year-old from Houston was playing, Navratilova was determined to beat her and claim a record ninth Wimbledon singles championship. She had lost the previous two Center Court finals to Graf, and in this, her incredible ninth straight Wimbledon final, Navratilova simply would not be denied. Garrison never had a chance.

To hone her game, especially the mental aspects of it, Navratilova had enlisted the services of six-time Wimbledon champ Billie Jean King before the tournament. The work paid off, as a calm, relaxed and efficient Navratilova cruised easily to the final. On Center Court, she steamrollered Garrison 6–4, 6–1 in 75 minutes. The match may have lacked the edge of Navratilova's classic nailbiters with Chris Evert or Graf, but its drama lay in what it meant for the record books.

The champion fell to her knees and then rushed to the grandstand to embrace her friend Judith Nelson and King before collecting her ninth silver plate, accompanied by a prim peck on the cheek from the Duchess of Kent.

IN SI'S WORDS

After fighting off one break point in the second game of the finals, Navratilova won 24 of 28 service points in an overwhelming display of grass-court aggression. Afterward she knelt in prayer, climbed into the guest box and kissed everyone save the Duchess of Fergie. Then the old—"I'm not a dinosaur," she said, but she is almost 34, fully 20 years older than [Jennifer] Capriati—and new champ paid tribute to the coaching of Billie Jean King, with whom she formed an alliance in May of last year. "She got my head straight last year when I didn't even know I was burnt out," Navratilova said. She also said, referring to her prolonged, single-minded pursuit of title No.9, that she had looked up the word "obsession" and found it meant irrational reverence. "I prefer to consider my love for Wimbledon a rational reverence," she said.

—Curry Kirkpatrick, July 16, 1990

Navratilova would not be denied in her quest for No. 9.

Sixty-One in '61

OCTOBER 1, 1961 "It would have been a hell of a lot more fun if I had never hit those 61 home runs," Roger Maris once said. "All it brought me was headaches."

In 1961 Maris and his Yankee teammate Mickey Mantle dared challenge Babe Ruth's single-season record of 60 home runs, set in 1927. Ruth was the most beloved Yankee of all time, and Mantle, too, was adored by New York fans. But Maris, in only his second season with the Yanks, was treated like an interloper.

After Mantle succumbed to injuries in September, Maris shouldered the burden alone. He was hounded in every city, by press and fans alike. "It would be a shame if Ruth's record got broken by a .270 hitter," said Hall of Famer Rogers Hornsby. Maris's hair began to fall out in clumps as the pressure intensified, but he kept hitting home runs at a record pace.

He'd hit 60 of them (*see sidebar*) when the Yankees met the Red Sox in New York for the final game of the season. In the fourth inning, Maris launched a 2–0 pitch from Tracy Stallard into the rightfield stands for his historic, bittersweet 61st home run of the year. Reluctantly, Maris stepped out of the dugout for a standing ovation from the crowd. "I think that Roger's feeling," said teammate Tony Kubek, "… was just relief, plain old-fashioned relief. He could relax now."

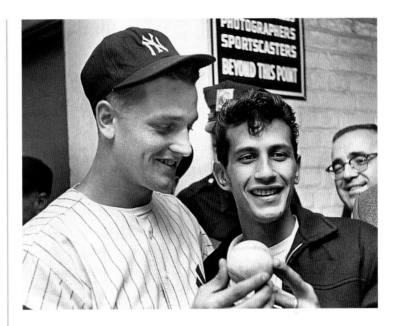

SPOTLIGHT

The American League expanded from eight to 10 teams in 1961, and as a result, the schedule grew from 154 to 162 games. In July of '61, when Roger Maris and Mickey Mantle were well ahead of Babe Ruth's record-setting home run pace of 1927, major league commissioner Ford Frick, who had been a close friend of Ruth's, made a controversial decision. Frick declared that if anyone was to break Ruth's record of 60 home runs, he would have to do so in 154 games, the length of the schedule in 1927. If Maris or Mantle surpassed 60 homers after the 154th game of the year, his season total would be accompanied by "some distinctive mark" or asterisk.

Frick's weighty asterisk would haunt Maris until his death of lymphatic cancer in 1985 at age 51. Six years after Maris's death, baseball officials removed the asterisk from the books and gave Maris his due. His record would last for 37 years—three years longer than Ruth's mark had stood.

Maris sent No. 61 (left) into the rightfield stands, where Sal Durante (above, with Maris) retrieved it.

One Giant Leap
For Mankind

OCTOBER 18, 1968 The world record in the long jump was 27'4¾" when Bob Beamon took his place at the top of the runway and contemplated his first attempt of the 1968 Olympic long jump final. Under gloomy skies he began his run, hit the board perfectly and soared higher than any jumper before. He hit the sand so hard he bounced right out of the end of the pit.

At first the judges tried to measure it with the newfangled sighting device running the length of the pit. But that stopped at 28 feet, so they had to use an old-fashioned steel measuring tape. The mark was posted in meters—8.90—leaving Beamon uncertain of what he'd done. "Bob, you jumped 29 feet!" his teammate Ralph Boston told him. In fact, it was 29'2½", and taking that in sent Beamon to his knees in what experts termed a "cataplectic seizure."

"Compared to this jump we are as children," said Igor Ter-Ovanesyan of Russia. "It is a mutation performance," said physiologist Ernst Jokl. "In the 33

From the look of things, some Mexico City officials missed the most amazing long jump ever.

"I can't go on. What is the point? We'll all look silly."

— British jumper Lynn Davies,
after Beamon's jump

IN SI'S WORDS

As the 400-meter finalists took the track, a rapidly approaching storm, the second of the day, was amassing thunderheads over the far side of the stadium. Against the enveloping clouds the inhabitants of the great bowl seemed to shine in a clear, unearthly light. The wind had not yet risen.

As they walked to the start, the three U.S. quartermilers, Lee Evans, Larry James and Ron Freeman, turned to watch a friend and teammate take his first try in the finals of the long jump. The man was Bob Beamon. He sprinted lightly down the runway and leapt.

From their angle the 400-meter men couldn't guess his distance, but Beamon had jumped so high that he performed his hitch kick and got his legs out in front while still about five feet above the pit. As he descended, he was like a majestic, prehistoric bird, suddenly awkward near the earth, landing hard.

Hope he didn't foul *that* one, thought Freeman, because Beamon was notorious for overrunning the board.

— Kenny Moore, June 29, 1987

years before 1968, the long jump record was only improved 8½ inches from Jesse Owens's 26' 8¼" in 1935. At that rate, Beamon's jump is an 84-year advance." Well, not quite. Beamon's mark stood unassailed until the arrival of Carl Lewis in the early '80s. Lewis came close on a number of occasions, but when the record finally fell, it was to Mike Powell, who leaped 29' 4½" in the 1991 world championships.

Beamon's aerial act (right) produced a hard landing (above) that bounced him straight out of the back of the pit.

The Bard of the Links

AUGUST 4, 1945 For five months in 1945 Byron Nelson made the world of professional golf his private domain. His legendary run of excellence began at the Miami Four Ball on March 8 and finished with a 10-stroke victory at the Canadian Open in Montreal in August. Nelson, a PGA veteran since '32, ruled the fairways—and the greens and the rough—during the 1945 season. He won 18 official tournaments and a record 11 in a row to cement one of the most remarkable years ever in golf. Skill coupled with a staunch focus drove Nelson's streak. "Winners," he once said, "are a different breed of cat. They ... are willing to give of themselves whatever it takes to win."

Consider Nelson's 19 consecutive rounds under 70; his final-round scoring average of 67.68; his seven second-place finishes and his average winning margin of 6.25 strokes in the 16 stroke-play events he won, and Nelson ascends to quasi-divine status, at least in golfing terms. After Nelson won the 1937 Masters, sportswriter O.B. Keeler nicknamed the golfer Lord Byron, because Nelson's back nine play reminded him of a Lord Byron poem. The moniker is hardly hyperbolic; after all, Nelson's record 11 straight tournament wins, like Byron's verse, may last forever.

AFTERMATH

With all due respect to Byron Nelson, the unbreakability of the record 11-tournament win streak he launched in 1945 may have more to do with the number of fiercely talented golfers currently on the Tour than with Nelson's undeniable prowess on the course. Given that, there have been modern streaks to rival Nelson's über-record. Ben Hogan, who caddied with Nelson at Fort Worth's Glen Garden Country Club in the '20s (both men are native Texans), won four straight in 1953 after recovering from a car accident that badly battered his legs and shoulders and fractured his pelvis. Forty-six years later, Tiger Woods tied Hogan's run.

As for Nelson, hemophilia and a burn-out pushed him out of the game one year after his famous streak. In 1946, he cashed in the war bonds he won as a player, purchased a ranch in Texas and retired.

Given the fierce competition on today's tour, Nelson's record may never be broken.

GREATEST MOMENTS

Big Mac

SEPTEMBER 8, 1998 It was an amazing thing to be part of, and yes, we all felt as if we were a part of it. Sure, it was Mark McGwire and Sammy Sosa who were actually bashing out all those home runs, closing in on Roger Maris's 37-year-old single-season record of 61. But, somehow, they were extensions of our collective will as we urged them on.

What made the whole thing even sweeter was that Sosa and McGwire seemed like great guys. They actually liked each other. Who else really knew what this kind of pressure—daily news conferences, constant scrutiny—was like?

By the All-Star break, McGwire had bashed 37 homers and Sosa, who'd knocked out 20 in July alone—a record—had 33. They fell off pace in early August but quickly rallied, and by Labor Day weekend, it was clear both would break Maris's mark. McGwire got there first, and he was lucky enough to do it at home, in St. Louis, against Sosa's Cubs. He tied the record on September 7 and broke it the next day with a line drive to left off Steve Trachsel. Sosa ran in from rightfield to offer congratulations, and an entire country celebrated its good fortune to be part of baseball's greatest summer. When the season finished, McGwire had stretched Maris's mark to an almost perverse 70, and Sosa totaled 66.

IN SI'S WORDS

When you sit down to tell the grandchildren the story, you might as well start out like this: Once upon a time.... For that is how all great fables begin. And when you do tell the tale ... you should be careful to linger over each detail of the ending, smiling to yourself at how preposterous it is that every last bit of it is true.

At 8:39 p.m. CDT on the last Friday of the season, McGwire didn't even have the most home runs in the National League Central, let alone the most ever in one season.... [In Houston] Sammy Sosa, the Chicago Cubs' redoubtable yang to McGwire's yin, had overtaken McGwire in a contest that resembled in its madness and score an NCAA basketball tournament game, 66–65. St. Louisans were aghast with fear. Even before the operator inside the Busch Stadium scoreboard replaced the 65 placard next to Sosa's name with a 66, McGwire ... knew what had happened. He could tell from the groans and murmurs of 48,159 fans. It was what anxiety sounds like.

— Tom Verducci, October 5, 1998

No. 62 was a looping liner to left off Steve Trachsel.

Wilt Goes for 100

MARCH 2, 1962 Comedian Adam Sandler once speculated on the conversations in the locker rooms at halftime of Wilt Chamberlain's astounding 100-point game against the Knicks:

New York player: "Who's guarding Chamberlain?"

Warriors player: "Wilt, I'm open."

Kidding aside, it didn't matter who was checking Wilt that night. He would not be denied. And his teammates had no complaints—four of them scored in double figures and they won the game by 22 points.

The Warriors probably weren't surprised, either. Chamberlain had been doing this all season. He *averaged* 50.4 points per game in 1961–62, which, needless to say, led the league. Only a month earlier Warrior Al Attles had said, "One day Wilt's going to score 100 points. Wait and see."

Who could have guessed the wait would be so short? Chamberlain's stats from the first quarter alone would have made for a stellar game: nine for nine from the free throw line, 23 points, 10 rebounds. The Warriors led 79–68 at the half, and Wilt had 41 points. Then he really got hot. Philadelphia pulled away to win 169–147, as Chamberlain poured in 31 points in the fourth quarter. A career .511 free-throw shooter, he was 28 for 32 from the line that night. There was definitely something in the air.

AFTERMATH

Wilt Chamberlain's 1961–62 season was one for the ages, unlikely ever to be matched. In addition to his 100-point game and his gaudy scoring and rebounding (25.7) averages, he became the first, and still only, player to top 4,000 points in a season, and he played every minute in 79 of his team's 80 games, also a record. Thanks to the seven overtime games the Warriors played that year, Chamberlain averaged 48.5 minutes per game—and NBA games are only 48 minutes long. He missed a paltry eight minutes of action all season.

The Warriors went 49–31, finishing second in the Eastern Division to the Boston Celtics, who set a record with 60 wins. The teams staged one of their epic battles in the Division Finals, trading victories until Game 7, when Boston guard Sam Jones hit a jumper with two seconds on the clock to give the Celtics a 109–107 win. Boston advanced to its fourth straight NBA Finals and defeated Los Angeles in seven games.

There was no television coverage of Chamberlain's record game, which was played in Hershey, Pa.

The Streak

SEPTEMBER 6, 1995 "If you could play baseball every day," the Baltimore Orioles' Cal Ripken Jr. once asked, "wouldn't you?"

Within that question lies the answer to what fueled Ripken on his immortal journey to break Lou Gehrig's record of 2,130 consecutive games played: his simple and abiding love of the game.

This was not a record fraught with sudden drama, seized in a breakthrough moment. This record was about preparation and craft and dedication—and, let's face it, a little luck. The Streak began on May 30, 1982, and ended on September 20, 1998, when Ripken took himself out of the Oriole lineup after 2,632 straight starts. He hadn't missed a game for 16½ seasons, and the consistency of his performance was almost metronomic. He was usually good for 25 homers and 90 RBIs a year, except in 1991, when he hit 34 dingers, drove in 114 runs and batted .323.

When Ripken eclipsed Gehrig in 1995, with his 2,131st consecutive start, he hit a home run in the fourth, and the sellout crowd in Baltimore's Camden Yards urged him to take a lap around the field when the game became official after the inning. He obliged, slapping hands with fans in the front rows as he circled the park. It was a sweet moment, one that helped baseball forget the nightmarish strike of '94.

IN SI'S WORDS

"What I really hate is that every time I get in a slump," Ripken said nine years ago, "they say it's because I'm tired from playing so much. Always, I'm tired. I'm not tired. It's not fair."

He was 25 years old when he said that, not yet one third of the way to eclipsing Lou Gehrig. He has played almost his entire career with people fussing so much about the Streak that they have missed the real artistry of the man. Take away the Streak and Ripken is still a Hall of Famer.

Cooperstown could cast an impressive plaque right now ... without ever mentioning the Streak: "No shortstop hit more home runs in a career ... or handled more consecutive chances flawlessly. He is the only player to start the All-Star Game in 12 consecutive years. A two-time MVP, he won the awards eight years apart, a span matched only by Joe DiMaggio and Willie Mays. He has played the game with intelligence, grace, passion, and, above all, respect."

—Tom Verducci, September 18, 1995

There was a festival atmosphere at Camden Yards on the night Ripken tied Gehrig.

The Grandest of Slams

SEPTEMBER 8, 1969 The late Arthur Ashe once likened Rod Laver's lethal left forearm to a "two-by-four with freckles." The Popeye–esque limb, which Laver developed on a homemade court in Queensland, Australia, may not have fit the 5'8½", 155-pound frame to which it was attached, but it gave Laver the most potent topspin groundstrokes tennis had ever seen.

In 1962 Laver became the second man (Don Budge was the first) to win tennis's Grand Slam, seizing the Australian, French, U.S. and Wimbledon titles. But when he turned pro in 1963, the four majors, clinging to their amateur ideals, banished him. By the time open tournaments were introduced in 1968, Laver had lost five years of his prime.

At the start of 1969, Laver, at 30, was determined to make up for lost time. "I went to Australia with [the Grand Slam] in mind," he said. He easily defeated Andres Gimeno for his third Australian title, then conquered fellow Aussies Ken Rosewall and John Newcombe to win the French Open and Wimbledon finals, respectively. Only the U.S. Open remained. In the final against Tony Roche, Laver adjusted to the rain by switching shoes and won in four sets. His unprecedented second Slam, the first of the open era, was complete.

IN SI'S WORDS

With Rod Laver, it is the eyes that give away his viciousness on the court, the cold, hollow, dilated pale blue eyes of an anxious fighting cock. They are not difficult to notice despite the Australian flop hat that covers the shock of red-blond hair and sallow face, covers everything except the beaked, sunburned nose. He has the hard face and the wiry, bowlegged body of a freckled Aussie sundowner who would be more at home on the ranch his father once owned than on the center court at Wimbledon or in the stadium at Forest Hills. But mainly it is the eyes that you return to, especially when he is down a service break and begins to scatter heavy, top-spun passing shots from his position of controlled nervousness and anger.

—Kim Chapin, August 26, 1968

Laver knocked off Roche at Forest Hills to become the only man ever to win two Grand Slams.

The Perfect Season

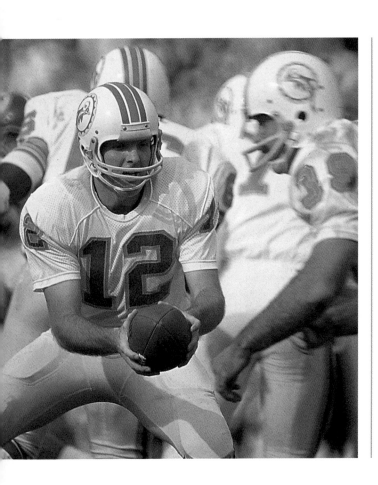

JANUARY 14, 1973 Sandwiched between the Green Bay Packer and Pittsburgh Steeler dynasties, the Dolphins of 1972 and '73 may well have been the most dominant NFL team ever. Under jut-jawed coach Don Shula, Miami ran up a cumulative record of 32–2 that included two Super Bowl titles and one perfect season, the only one of its kind in league history.

The Dolphins had a wonderfully balanced offense, in which the threat of Bob Griese's deadly passes offered cover for a punishing running game powered by Larry Csonka, Jim Kiick and Mercury Morris. Miami ran off 16 straight wins, including tidy playoff victories over Cleveland (20–14) and Pittsburgh (21–17), to get to Super Bowl VII against Washington.

If the Dolphins felt the pressure of being on the verge of the unprecedented, you couldn't tell. They were a model of efficiency and poise. Griese passed only 11 times, but completed eight for 88 yards and one

Griese (left) handed off to Csonka (right) 15 times for 112 yards in Super Bowl VII.

"I like to run where there's holes, Larry likes to run where there's people."

—Jim Kiick,
on his backfield
partner Larry Csonka

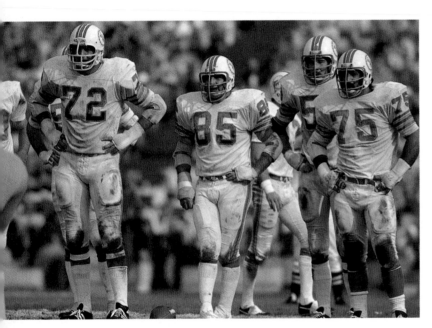

IN SI'S WORDS

It was not always easy, and far less dramatic than it might have been, but the Miami Dolphins finally demonstrated rather conclusively that they are the biggest fish in the pro football pond. In the seventh Super Bowl they defeated the Washington Redskins 14–7 before 81,706 sweltering and smog-beset fans in the Los Angeles Memorial Coliseum. This meant that the Dolphins went an entire season without a loss, 17 straight. No other NFL team has ever gone undefeated for a season, and no other club is likely to do it again soon, either. On the record, then, Miami is the best club in pro football history.

touchdown. Csonka rushed for 112 yards on 15 carries. And the Miami defense stifled the 'Skins, intercepting three passes and shutting out their offense. Washington only scored in the waning minutes, when Miami kicker Garo Yepremian picked up a blocked field-goal attempt and made a comical-looking pass attempt. Mike Bass intercepted and ran it back for a touchdown. But you need a little comic relief in the midst of such awesome perfection.

The Dolphins won the game with a nearly impeccable first half; with an extraordinarily accurate passer in quarterback Bob Griese; with a rhino of a runner, Larry Csonka; and, above all, with a defense that may have been No Names, but was plenty of adjectives. Try tough, tight, dashing and daring for starters.

—Tex Maule, January 22, 1973

Yepremian's gaffe (right) added a touch of comedy to the end of Miami's perfect season, but the Dolphins' legendary No-Name Defense (above) certainly did not find it funny.

Honorable Mention

THE DRIVE Chapter One in the NFL book of Elway: a 98 ½-yard march in the 1986 AFC title game against Cleveland. Elway survived an eight-yard sack, escaped a third-and-18 jam and passed for the tying score with 37 seconds left. Then he did it again in overtime to set up the 33-yard field goal that put Denver in Super Bowl XXI.

YOUNG MASTER Jack Nicklaus won the 1963 Masters at age 23. Just a cub at the time, the Golden Bear shot a 2-under 286 to win by one stroke over Tony Lema.

MAN U. TRIPLE Having already won the English Premier League title as well as the F.A. Cup, Manchester United trailed Bayern Munich 1–0 in stoppage time of the 1999 European Cup final. The Red Devils got an equalizer, from Teddy Sheringham, and before pub denizens the world over could order another pint for overtime, Ole Gunnar Solskjaer scored to complete a historic triple.

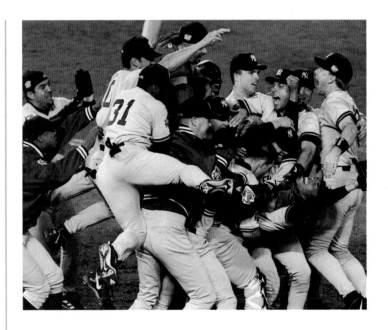

THAT 125-WIN SEASON Highlighted by Mark McGwire and Sammy Sosa's riveting home-run race, 1998 was a baseball season for the ages. And it ended, fittingly, with a 24th World Series title for the Yankees, who won a record 125 games.

El Duque and the 1998 Yankees may have been the best team ever.

ONWARD CHRISTIAN SOLDIER

Trailing Kentucky 103–102, Duke had the ball with 2.1 seconds left in overtime of the 1992 NCAA East Regional final. Grant Hill slung a 75-foot pass to Christian Laettner, who caught the ball near the top of the key, dribbled once, turned and drained his shot as the buzzer sounded, sending the Blue Devils to the Final Four.

HOYA DESTROYAS Shooting a white-hot 79% from the field, eighth-seeded Villanova upset defending champion and No. 1 seed Georgetown 66–64 to win the 1985 NCAA basketball title.

ROCKET-FUELED When Maurice (Rocket) Richard passed away on May 27, 2000, all Canada mourned, and heads of state, NHL legends and hundreds of citizens attended his funeral. They celebrated the first shooting star of the NHL, the man who scored a landmark 50 goals in 50 games in 1944–45.

TRAILBLAZER In September of 1968 Arthur Ashe became the first, and still only, African-American man to win the U.S. Open tennis singles title, outlasting Tom Okker in five sets. Ashe smashed 26 aces in the triumph.

EXTRA SWEET They called him Sweetness, and on November 20, 1977, Chicago Bears back Walter Payton was sweeter than ever. Against the Minnesota Vikings he carried 40 times for 275 yards, an NFL record.

THE IRON HORSE SAYS GOODBYE

Suffering from amyotrophic lateral sclerosis, the disease that now bears his name, Lou Gehrig made his immortal retirement speech to New York fans on July 4, 1939, a day the Yankees set aside in his honor. "You may have been reading about a bad break I got," he began, his words echoing off the Yankee Stadium facades. . . .

Laettner (top), Gehrig (above) and Payton (right) all created immortal sports moments.

BUCKY DENTS BOSTON Bucky Dent hit only five home runs in 1978, but his fifth was one Boston Red Sox fans will never forget. It looked like a harmless pop fly until it drifted over the Green Monster in left to carry the Yankees to victory in a one-game AL East playoff.

MAGIC SHOW A 6'9" rookie point guard, Magic Johnson of the Lakers filled in for an injured Kareem Abdul-Jabbar at *center* in Game 6 of the 1980 NBA Finals against Philadelphia. Eventually playing every position on the court, Johnson scored 42 points, grabbed 15 rebounds and made seven assists as he led Los Angeles to the title.

"ZÁ-TO-PEK, ZÁ-TO-PEK" With the huge stadium crowd chanting his name, Czech distance runner Emil Zátopek cruised to victory in the marathon at the 1952 Olympics. His amazing versatility made him the toast of the Helsinki Games: Zátopek had already won the 5,000 and the 10,000, and he set three Olympic records.

TOUR DE LANCE Only 21 months removed from testicular cancer, Lance Armstrong of the U.S. won the 1999 Tour de France, cycling's most grueling race.

NICKED KNICK An injured Willis Reed, the Knicks captain, hobbled out for Game 7 of the 1970 NBA Finals against the Lakers and hit his first two shots, inspiring New York to a 113–99 victory.

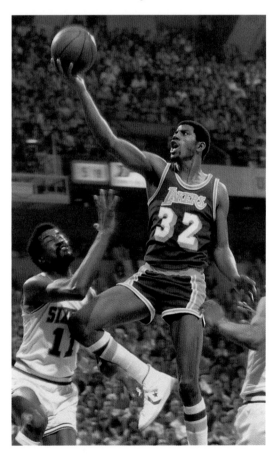

Armstrong (left) and Zátopek (top) showed grit and endurance, while Johnson (above) was pure magic.

Photo Credits

Index